BETTER THA

BETTER THAN THE WITCH DOCTOR

Mary Cundy

MONARCH
Crowborough

First published 1994

British Library Cataloguing in Publication Data
A catalogue record for this book is available
from the British Library.

ISBN 1 85424 267 9

Designed and produced in England for
MONARCH PUBLICATIONS
Broadway House, The Broadway, Crowborough,
East Sussex TN6 1HQ by
Nuprint Ltd, Station Road, Harpenden, Herts AL5 4SE.

CONTENTS

CHRONOLOGY

1935 Nepal Border Fellowship
Kitty Harbord visits Tansen
Lily O'Hanlon and Hilda Steele come to
Nautanwa

1951 Lily O'Hanlon and Hilda Steele invited to
Kathmandhu

1951 Dr Carl Friedericks and Flemings' trip to Nepal
Dr Carl Friedericks and Flemings invited to
open hospitals in Tansen and Kathmandhu

1957 Mary goes to Tansen

1960 Hilda Steele goes to Pyersingh

1962 Mary returns from leave and sent out on
survey

1967 Mary goes to Pyersingh to join Hilda
Paimey dispensary starts

1970 Pastor Narhu becomes pastor of Pyersingh in
Paimey Church

1972 Hilda retires. Mary operated on for cancer

1973 Hilda and Mary return to Paimey

1975 Mary takes over Paimey dispensary
Hilda comes home

1989 Mary comes home and Prabhu Dan and Jyoti
take over Paimey Dispensary

PREFACE

This book could also be called 'The price of freedom'. It tells the story of the Christian church in Nepal from the time when Nepal was a closed land where no Christians were allowed, to 1991 when Christmas Day was proclaimed a public holiday.

Christ was crucified and then rose from the dead. It is not a glib statement to say, 'No cross, no crown.' We have seen this principle worked out in the history of the Nepali church. This is, too, my personal story, which I was asked to write. I pray that in the telling of this story, you will come to love and respect the hardy people of Nepal. I pray, too, that your faith, or lack of it, will be challenged–mine certainly was during the thirty-three years I had the privilege of living among them.

ACKNOWLEDGEMENTS

My grateful thanks to:

Valerie Heard who typed the manuscript on to computer disc;

Dr Tom Hale for his encouragement, help and advice;

Pamela Winnett and my many prayer partners without whose help and support I would not have survived.

FOREWORD

In 1957 a young English social worker named Mary Cundy left her homeland and journeyed to the fabled kingdom of Nepal, where for the next thirty-three years she served the Nepali people in some of the most remote and difficult areas of the country. For most of her time in Nepal, Mary lived a day's walk from the nearest road, high in the Himalayan foothills. She lived at the level of the impoverished villagers, sharing in their hardships, their sorrows and their joys.

Though she had no formal medical training, Mary started a dispensary, and within a short time was seeing up to 100 patients a day, many of them desperately ill. Yet, over a period of three decades, no patient ever died under her care. The only times a patient ever died were the rare occasions when a medical doctor happened to be visiting Mary. This is not an indictment of the medical profession; rather, it is a testimony to the remarkable way in which God blessed Mary's healing ministry through all those years. Thousands of Nepalis today owe their lives to Mary.

But Mary would say, correctly, that those Nepalis owe their lives to God. Everything Mary did was done in dependence upon God. Day after day she proved God's faithfulness, even in the midst of impossible circumstances. And over and over God enabled, often in marvellous and unexpected ways. Mary's work was not limited to physical healing. She was equally

involved in spiritual healing, evangelism and discip-
ling, and taking on the powers of darkness and evil
that keep the Nepali people in bondage. She led in the
formation of a church in her area, which has steadily
grown in spite of intense opposition from the surrounding community. And today Mary's work is being
carried on: a Christian Nepali couple are running the
dispensary, and a Nepali pastor leads the church.

Mary's life is an illustration of how God takes
ordinary people and turns them into extraordinary
people. Mary does not have peculiar qualifications
that the rest of us don't have; she simply obeyed
God's call to serve him in Nepal–and she kept on
obeying. And, as always, God honoured that obedience, and he used Mary to accomplish great things in
Nepal many of which are recorded in this book.

This is Mary's story, a story of adventure, heartache, joy, struggle, and perseverance. It is told with
self-effacement, honesty and humour. It is my hope
that many will read this book, and be inspired to
follow Mary's example–to dare to trust God and to
obey him. Those who commit their lives to God are
never disappointed. Mary has proven the truth of
Jesus' statement: 'no one who has left home or
brothers or sisters or mother or father or children or
fields for me and the gospel will fail to receive a hundred times as much in this present age (homes,
brothers, sisters, mothers, children and fields–and
with them, persecutions) and in the age to come, eternal life' (Mk 10:29-30, NIV). Today, in 'retirement'
back in England, Mary is rich beyond reckoning.

Thomas Hale

1

Nepal, Here We Come!

The bus standing at Sonauli, a ramshackle checkpoint on the Nepal-India border would hardly pass the M.O.T.! That it held together at all was a tribute to Nepali ingenuity. The bus had wooden seats with no padding and no glass in the windows except in the driver's cabin.

It was 1957. Carl and Betty Anne Friedericks, two of their children, Chucky and Jimmy (aged four and two), and I were crammed in with the driver in his cabin. It was only after much argument that we had managed to get ourselves and our luggage in at all. There were about fifty other people as well as goats on a vehicle built to take half that number. I was to learn that Nepali buses never went until they were full—that is, until no more people, luggage or livestock could be squeezed inside, outside or on top.

This, however, was my first trip. I had arrived in India by boat some months previously during the first Suez crisis, a journey of one month from Liverpool to Bombay. I had then gone to learn Nepali in Mussoorie, North India, where I had met the Friedericks and heard I was to work with them in Tansen, Nepal.

We had come together on the overnight train from Gorakhpur to Nautanwa, the last railhead in India, arriving there at 3.30 am. There were no waiting-room facilities so we lay on the platform until dawn. Then began a memorable journey. The first part of the journey was a twenty-five-mile bus trip to the border post of Sonauli. Sonauli at that time was no more than a check and customs post, surrounded by a group of mud huts that served as resting places for travellers.

It was the end of the rains—hot, damp and muggy and we were eager to get through customs on the Indian and Nepali sides of the border as quickly as possible. We had, however, to clear our mountain of luggage. The fact that Carl was well known as the Doctor Sahib who was starting a hospital in Tansen helped, but did not eliminate the string of questions as to what was in the various boxes, containers and cases we had with us.

Surrounded by curious people all wanting to see and hear everything, I remember my embarrassment when the large number of packets of sanitary towels (we were told to take a three or four years' supply!) were revealed, one customs man, in the know, restraining the other from asking what they were used for. Then at last when everyone's patience was wearing thin, after much filling in of forms, in duplicate, which had to be checked, all the luggage was cleared. Carl said, 'Come on, grit your teeth for the next part of the journey' as we made our way to find the bus.

So here we were, waiting, hoping, praying it would get us by nightfall as far as Butwal, a town in the foothills of Nepal and the next stage in our journey.

I had Jimmy, the younger boy, on my lap. Jimmy's mother, Betty Anne, was beside me by the window with Chucky on her knee. The engine was already belching fumes as the driver made efforts to start. I was just thinking, 'However am I going to endure this?' when Betty Anne broke into my thoughts with 'Jimmy usually heaves up on this trip!'

It was hot in that front cabin and we were tired. I looked round at the cramped accommodation and thought, 'Horrors, the only place he can heave up is on me.' In desperation I uttered the first of many spontaneous prayers I was to say during my thirty-three years in Nepal, 'Lord, please don't let Jimmy be sick until we get to Butwal.'

The driver finally managed to start the bus, and we lumbered slowly along the road leading from the border to the Nepali foothills. The mud-surfaced road would normally have been hot and dusty, but this was September and the end of the monsoon. There were still pools of water everywhere, and the road was full of potholes, making it very difficult for the driver. But he was undaunted and seemed to enjoy the challenge. The engine kept breaking down, to be mended with bits of bent wire. We also kept stopping to collect water for the radiator.

We had stopped many times before we reached Bhairawa, the only town on the way to Butwal. Here we stayed while the driver had his meal of rice and curry. We took on more passengers and luggage and mercifully unloaded some too. The only timetable seemed to be that the bus would start when it was overfull, then proceed as best it could to reach its destination some time. In Nepali philosophy, there is always tomorrow.

Bhairawa even in those days boasted an airport, with flights to the capital Kathmandu, to Pokhara in West Nepal, and one or two other destinations. But you certainly needed a flexible timetable to travel this way. I once waited from Monday to Thursday for a plane to Kathmandu, and in the end only got there because Carl knew the pilot and asked him to do a special unscheduled flight to pick up freight and collect my three companions and me. I nearly hugged the pilot when he arrived.

There was, however, to be no luxury of plane travel for us today; we were stuck with the bus. The unsurfaced road led along level land, with small mud huts and villages here and there, interspersed with stretches of dense jungle. People were beginning to move on to the road, starting cafes and small shops, putting up 'lean-to' shacks in which to sell their wares to the new customers coming into Nepal. It had been a closed land until 1951.

We lost count of the number of times the bus broke down. There were, of course, no toilet facilities, the side of the road being used for this purpose—much easier for men than for women. In later years I usually travelled in a wide skirt and carried a large black umbrella. I found it useful for more purposes than shielding from sun and rain!

We trundled on our way, and by evening arrived at Butwal at the base of the first foothills. As we came long the last stretch of road we had our first glimpse of the Himalayas, rising to 29,000 feet, specially memorable on that occasion as there was a rainbow over them, to me a token of God's unbreakable promises. Following the rainbow was a most beautiful sunset, bathing the high snow-capped mountain peaks with an orange glow. The austere grandeur of the Himalayas remain a gripping experience for most of us, but the first sight is always breathtaking. Majesty and mystery are mingled there. The call of the unknown, spectacularly beautiful yet compelling and sinister; no wonder the Nepalis called them the dwelling-place of the gods.

However, we had no time then to admire the view or muse on the great unknown. We had to climb out of the cabin, stretch weary limbs, and find porters to take our luggage to the dirty, uncomfortable house where we were to spend the night. In the middle of this confusion of scrambling porters, animals and people, Jimmy heaved up! His first time on the trip.

Although people from the hills came down to Butwal to buy salt for themselves and their animals and to collect their yearly supplies, the town was far from prosperous. Those who lived there, however, were better off than most hill people. Carl and Betty Anne had stayed there before, so they took us to a house that served as an inn. It had one large room downstairs with a mud floor, with maize-straw mats on which travellers could sleep. We were given an upstairs balcony to ourselves, with the doubtful privilege of straw sleeping-mats on wooden beds. I learned later in my travels in Nepal to avoid sleeping on such beds, if possible. At this stage, however, I was ignorant of the many sleepless nights I would spend with bed bugs.

Carl slept well that night, but there was little sleep for Betty Anne and me. We had not only bed bugs to cope with but also sleepless children. At the end of the balcony was a piece of tin sheeting to block the wind. It kept blowing down in the night, so we constantly had to get up to replace it. Carl woke the next morning, blissfully ignorant of our night's adventures, and was ready to go. He said we should leave at 7 am.

First, however, we had to find twelve Nepalis to carry our luggage on their backs (the only means of transportation in the hills). Our luggage included a primus stove, a deck chair (no comfy chairs in Tansen I was told, bring your own), and a tin bath tub (which later became a coveted possession since it was the only one big enough to sit down in), and six-months' supply of toilet paper! Beside our own luggage we also had supplies for the hospital, food, and other things we could not buy in Nepal. This took time to organise, so we did not set off until 9 am. We also had a horse, sent from Tansen, the town to which we were going, and there was a basket to be carried on a man's back for the boys to sit in turn by turn.

So off we went, a long cavalcade of people, Betty Anne on the horse with one of the boys, the other boy carried in a basket, Carl and I walking, and the twelve carriers bringing up the rear.

Butwal town is built on two sides of a swiftly flowing river at the entrance of a steep gorge. We set off walking between some well-built houses with tin roofs on either side of the road, which soon petered out, to be replaced by mud huts and poorly built shacks.

Soon our path took a drop down and we found ourselves clambering over large boulders and trying to keep on a precariously narrow path, very uneven and undulating, that ran by the side of the river. I wrote later: 'I would not have thought so much awful road could go on for so long.' It took us three to four hours to negotiate our way through the gorge, over boulders and slippery stones, sometimes going down level with the river, only to have to climb back up again over shifting rocks. At many places it was not possible for Betty Anne to ride the horse so when we at last reached the first village at the end of the gorge, she was not feeling well and had to lie down to recover.

There is now a bridge at Dhoban, and a motor road goes through the village, but then there was nothing, and we had to cross the river. I can remember us standing and looking at the water, swollen with the rains, flowing swiftly between boulders, over a wide and stony bed. Some Nepali men, with very heavy loads, were struggling over, skilled through long experience. Their baskets would be packed with the things that would not spoil in water, at the bottom, wrapped in plastic.

As Carl had a cine camera he wanted us to go first, so Chucky went over on the horse with the horseboy and Jimmy, protesting, in the basket on the porter's back. We watched them safely over. Now it was Betty Anne's and my turn. Carl found a Nepali to carry us across. Betty Anne is much smaller and lighter than I am. He got over safely with her. It was now my turn. I am tall and heavy. I climbed onto his back and we set off. All went well until we got to the middle of the river. Then his foot slipped and we lurched over. He, poor man, did his best to right himself, not easy with a heavy load on his back. I tried to help him, though it is difficult to know what to do in those circumstances. Mercifully he got himself upright again and we literally staggered over to the bank where we clambered out.

Then Carl came on over with the cine camera, expressing delight at the good pictures we had given him!

In India I had been given what was then considered to be an essential piece of missionary equipment, a pith helmet for protection against the sun. After my tumble in the river the hat had come off and I felt I just could not wear it any longer, so gave it to the horse-boy, who wore it with great pride for a number of years. I never had one again in all my years in Nepal as they ceased to be recommended headgear.

Of course, I was now soaked through. I had no change of clothes, so hoping I would dry off as I walked, I started trudging up the next part of the journey which was like a staircase made of large stone boulders. The trail led through a thick forest and I became more and more weary and breathless as I struggled upwards. I found myself all alone. The carriers were behind, Carl and Betty Anne, the horseboy, and the children had gone on far ahead.

I sat down heavily on a rock by the roadside wondering why I had come to Nepal. Writing later, I said: 'By 3 pm I did not care whether I lived or died. My only consolation was the movie Carl had taken of the early part of the trip. I thought it would make a good missionary appeal for someone to replace me if I died!'

I do not know how long I sat there, feeling I could not take another step, and that death was preferable to this. Long enough, however, for Carl to worry about my non-appearance further up. He sent down the horseboy and the horse; Betty Anne was feeling better by now. I gratefully clambered on. Sitting on the horse's back there seemed more air, and I began to feel better. We eventually reached, by evening, a village which consisted of one long cobbled street, with houses of mud and thatch on either side. All the houses had verandahs, and most were inns offering food and accommodation to the many Nepalis going down to Butwal from their mountain homes for supplies.

We stayed in the house of a lady who had gained

notoriety because she owned a teapot, an unheard of thing in those days. Through the years she was known to us as 'the lady with the teapot'. We all, including the porters, slept together in one room. Straw mats were provided and on these we spread our sleeping bags and pillows. We westerners were, of course, a novelty and half the village turned up to watch what we did. The lady of the house did her best, but eyes looked in through the cracks in the walls, windows and door. Everything was of interest. Toothbrushes were unknown in Nepal at that time. The Nepalis used a type of stick. So cleaning our teeth was a special event. Washing tended to be public, so the minimum was done, with all your clothes on. There is a real art to be learnt–how to wash discreetly, all over, in a stream or at a village water source. Going to the 'loo' with an audience is also an art to be learnt. I was never able to brazen it out. Having company for everything was a new experience for me that night. I grew used to this over the years; where I worked white people were always a rarity. It made me appreciate space and privacy even more–our need for this was something most Nepalis at that time did not understand.

In the morning, Betty Anne and I took it in turns on the horse, although I was rarely to travel by horse after this. Chucky and Jimmy alternated being on the horse with us, or riding in a basket on one of the men's backs. We went on over a 5,000 feet mountain, down the other side, waded across a small river and then on a narrow path by the side of the river. At one point we turned the corner and looked up and saw across the valley, nestling on the top of a 4,500 feet mountain, a small town. 'There's Tansen,' said Carl. It looked miles away. 'How to get there?' I thought. We certainly had further to go on the same path and then across rice fields until we reached the last hill up to Tansen.

It was evening by the time we arrived, the last stretch being very steep and tiring. After staggering up the hill, with many rests on the way, we came out on to a large green, flat open space. This was known as the Tundekhal. Here official town functions were held, the army paraded and sports were played.

As we walked round from the Tundekhal, we got a glimpse of one of the main streets in Tansen. On each side of the cobbled road were well-built two-storied houses, many with the wood carvings for which one of the Nepali castes, the Newars, are famous. The shops had slats across the front and these, when lifted out, opened up the room from which goods were sold. Apart from local grains, these were mostly imported from India.

Tansen is the administrative centre of the Palpa District and a medieval town. It had three schools, and a prison which we had passed on our way up. As well as having the Governor's house, it was also a religious centre and there were many Hindu temples. One of them was guarded by many bats which could be seen hanging upside down in the surrounding trees. There was also a Buddhist temple. Hindus and Buddhists seemed to attend each other's ceremonies. There was a very small Muslim minority and they had a small mosque in the upper part of the town.

There were lovely views of the Fish Tail mountain and Annapurna range from the Tundekhal. Every Nepali who could, it seemed, had turned out to look at us as we trudged wearily around the corner to a long, dirty, double-storey building. A verandah stood on each side of a central front door, leading up to which were eight wide steps. This was the building in which Carl had started the hospital, and it was still functioning there when I arrived. Hearing of our arrival, the hospital staff came out to greet us; beside Nepalis, there were three Swedes, one Norwegian, one Welsh and three English.

I was not expected, so there was no room or bed for me. I began my life in Tansen lying on the floor in a shared bedroom.

2

The Call

Missionary life held no illusions for the Friedericks, who had been in China when the communists came. Turned out of China, they had gone to India. In 1951 Carl had joined two fellow Americans, Drs Bob and Bethel Fleming, on a trip to Nepal. This trip had followed one made by Dr Bob, an ornithologist, in 1949. He had been asked by the Chicago Museum of Natural History to go to Nepal to study birds. At that time Nepal was a closed and isolated land. It was ruled by the Ranas, a family of hereditary prime ministers who had usurped power from the royal family a century earlier. When Carl went in 1951, a revolution had occurred, led by King Tribhuvan. He had overthrown the Rana government and taken power into his own hands. Prior to this he had lived virtually as a prisoner in his own palace. But when he became ruler, King Tribhuvan opened Nepal to the outside world and established His Majesty's Government.

Nepal had had very little contact with western medicine at this time, most people relying on help from witch doctors. These 'doctors' relied on local herbal remedies, but also taught that diseases were caused by evil spirits. To 'cure' the patient, they said incantations to the Hindu gods and demanded sacrifices to appease them so that the patient could get better. These sacrifices would often be a chicken or, for a serious condition, a goat.

While Bob Fleming was searching for his birds, his wife Bethel and Carl, both medical doctors, found they were kept busy with unofficial patients. Everywhere they went they attracted large crowds, and they quickly began to realise the tremendous medical needs of the Nepali people.

After some time, requests came from the Nepal government for the Flemings and the Friedericks to open hospitals in the capital, Kathmandu, and in Tansen, a trade centre in West Nepal. The Flemings (Methodists) were asked to go to Kathmandu and the Friedericks (Presbyterians) to Tansen.

Both their mission boards realised that while the invitation was personal to the two families, the proposed medical work would require two teams working together, and large resources. The boards also felt that this was not something God was leading the two couples into alone, nor was it to be limited only to the Americans. So they invited missions worldwide to join. Among those who responded was an interdenominational English mission, Zenana Bible and Medical Mission, later the Bible and Medical Missionary Fellowship, now called Interserve.

An elderly, saintly friend used to say that the links God gave his children are amazing. I am an only child and my father died eighteen days after the 1939 war broke out. I was evacuated with my school to Caversham, Reading. As it was war time, my uncle, a Church of England clergyman, was made my guardian on father's death. He wrote to Enid Gilkes, the local leader of Crusaders (an interdenominational Bible class) asking her to invite me to the class. This she did, and she befriended me when I really needed it. Besides attending the class, I was also confirmed in the local Church of England. I was teased about this at school, and in 1941 when I moved back to London, I decided I was going to have nothing more to do with religion.

However Enid, who by this time was not living in Reading, invited me to go to a Crusader camp in Seascale, Cumbria. Largely to please her, and because it was an opportunity in war time for a holiday, I decided to go. The decision was to have a far-reaching effect on my life.

At the camp I fended off various people who asked about the condition of my soul! Then one evening I was sitting in the meeting room of the school overlooking the sea at Seascale, lost in my own thoughts. One of the leaders was speaking and reading 1 John 5:10–'He that believes on the Son of God has the witness in himself, he that believes not God has made Him a liar, because he believes not in the record that God gave of His Son.'

It was as if God was speaking to me alone in that room. He said, 'Mary, so you are going to call me a liar for the rest of your life?' It was a decisive moment, and I knew that I could not look God in the face and call him a liar. I had no choice but to accept or reject the truth. There was no middle way. I knew God had spoken to me.

The next day Enid and I were walking by the sea. She urged me to ask Jesus into my life, and mark a verse in my Bible to seal that I had done so. I did just that. I went back to the dormitory, knelt down and asked Jesus to come into my life and save me. The verse I marked was Acts 2:21–'Whosoever shall call on the name of the Lord shall be saved.' When tempted to doubt my salvation, I could point to that verse and say, 'I called; he is faithful to his promise, and whatever I may feel like, he saved me.'

In April 1955 my mother died. I now had no family ties. I was, however, happily established and enjoying my chosen career. I was Head Medical Social Worker at the Royal Berkshire Hospital, Reading.

Dr Patricia Strong of Raxaul, India, hearing of my mother's death, wrote suggesting I go to work in India. I replied that I was too old at thirty, could not learn a language, and was hopeless in the heat (all perfectly true)! As far as I was concerned, it was a closed door. Amazingly, however, all through that summer of 1955 the little-known land of Nepal kept coming to my attention.

People put leaflets through my door. A friend met someone who worked there who could not stop talking about Nepal. There were television and radio programmes about Nepal, as well as newspaper and magazine articles. For me, however, the most surprising thing that happened was when I went to help at a Christian camp in Wales.

I decided to contact a fellow medical social worker with whom I had worked and invite her to supper. We had not met for several years and she knew nothing of what I was going through. When she came she said, 'Mary, it's interesting you should get in touch with me now, as I was thinking of you. A friend of mine has just been the doctor on an Everest expedition and he told me there is a need for social workers in Nepal. I thought of you, as you were friendly with Trevor and Patricia Strong who went to work up on the Nepal border. (I had forgotten we had all worked together.)

You would be so much more use in Nepal than me, as you are a Christian and I'm not!'

When I got back from the holiday, there was a letter from Patricia Strong, ignoring what I had written to her and suggesting I apply for the newly-opened land of Nepal. She even mentioned the three missions who were then working in Nepal: Nepal Evangelistic Band, Regions Beyond Missionary Union, and Zenana Bible and Medical Mission. I began to wonder if God was calling me to Nepal. I knelt down by my bed before going to church and prayed the words of an old hymn: 'Speak to me by name, O Master, let me know it is to me.'

The second lesson in church contained the words: 'I count all things but loss' (Phil 3:8). It was as if, as I sat there, God said to me, 'Mary, are you willing to count all things but loss?' I thought about my flat, my friends, my career, and I said, 'No God, I am not willing.' A little later John Page, my vicar at Greyfriars, Reading, got up to preach. He said, 'I have three words for my text today. "For my sake." They are taken from Mark 10:29. Jesus said, "There is no-one that has left house or brethren or sister or father or mother or children or lands for my sake and the Gospel's but he shall receive a hundredfold now in this time, house and brethren and sisters and mothers and children and lands with persecutions and in the world to come eternal life." '

As I sat there, it was as if Jesus took these two verses and put them together and said, 'Mary, are you not willing, for my sake, to count all things but loss?' I said, 'But Lord, you can't pin that verse on me. I do not have any family.' God said, 'Look down at your Bible.' I looked, and gently he said, 'What comes first? House.

You have a home, so that verse does apply to you.' So it went on until I was pretty certain I had to apply somewhere for work in Nepal. But where to begin?

Well, Patricia had mentioned three societies. I knew that the Nepal Evangelistic Band already had a social worker. I knew nothing about Regions Beyond Missionary Union apart from knowing the Strongs, who were missionaries with them. However, I did know the Zenana Bible and Medical Mission as we supported it in the Crusader class I ran. We were also taking a group to one of their meetings the next week. At that meeting, the only place for which help was asked was Nepal!

I wrote to Jack Dain, the General Secretary, asking if there would be any use for a social worker in Nepal. Jack replied that before opening my letter he had opened one from Nepal, asking for a team to go to a new place, and to include someone like a social worker. This never actually happened, but it was still used to nudge me on.

No call is without its testings. My first test came when I was filling in the ZBMM medical form. I had had ear trouble, and my ear specialist said he had been in the army in India and had turned down people with my condition. He added, however, that if I did not mention it, I might get there without them finding out. But I knew I had to tell ZBMM what he had said, and wondered whether I would be turned down on my ears.

ZBMM arranged for me to see another ear specialist in Wimpole Street. To me it was significant that the Nepalese Ambassador was one of his patients, so he knew all about the then little-known land of Nepal. He examined my ears and said, 'Had you been going to

India, I would have turned you down, but as you are hoping to go to Nepal I can say that you will be no liability to the society.'

My second testing came over my furniture. My mother had died shortly after we moved to Reading, and I was living in a hospital flat. This was to be a temporary measure while we looked for a house. I had to give three months notice from my job, and be out of the flat, too, in that time. I felt I should not sell the furniture. I knew I would not be able to afford to store it, but what to do with it?

One month passed and I had no solution; two months, and still nothing. I have found that God keeps us cliff-hanging on these occasions. He does, of course, say that the trial of our faith is more precious than gold (1 Pet 1:5). My faith, by this time, was being sorely tried.

Then I met John Page, my vicar, in the corridor of the hospital. He asked me how I was. I said, 'Well, I think I will be sitting in the middle of London Road (where I lived) surrounded by my furniture in a month's time.' John said, 'Oh, we will make it a special matter at the prayer meeting tonight.'

The next morning, a friend phoned to say that she had heard I had a flat full of furniture and nowhere to store it, whereas she, at the end of the month, was going to have a house and no furniture! Her friend had just got a new job and was moving and taking all the furniture with her. So, to the day, it fitted. At the end of the month, my furniture went to her empty house. Another thing my saintly friend used to say was, 'God often leaves it until the last train, but he never misses it.' Neither did he this time.

My furniture gone, my job given up, my bridges burnt—what next?

As I had taken the London University Certificate of Religious Knowledge and also courses at the London Bible College, I was only asked to go to St Michael's House, Oxford, for two terms. This was to see, the Mission said, if other people could live with me and I with them! A Bible College is a great testing place for this. I never heard the verdict on this, but here I was in Nepal, all set to try and put into practice what I had learnt on unsuspecting missionary colleagues and Nepalis.

3

So To Work

I joined the other Mission personnel living in the house Carl had rented from a whiskery old Brahmin who lived next door. His family were priests to the king of Nepal. The wooden buildings were rambling and ramshackle. We lived upstairs and the hospital was downstairs. It could house about twelve in-patients, but always had many more. Relatives and friends of patients usually stayed with them. They often slept on straw mats they had brought with them, which they laid out on the mud floor under the patient's bed.

One of my first impressions, and something I never got used to, was the Nepalis' habit of clearing their throats and then making a loud spit! They would do this daily under my bedroom window, especially early in the morning.

I shared a bedroom for a while, until the room used as a prayer/guest/meeting/language room was partitioned to make a bedroom too. I wrote: 'This place is a rabbit warren and has everything to try mind, body and spirit—no real privacy, awful sanitation (a hole in the ground outside), oil lamps which either smoke or don't light, dripping candles, people of differing opinions and background in every way, heat, dirt, mosquitoes, leeches, snakes, and rats—the latter abounding.'

The room I was given was to be my office as well as my bedroom. It was next to the storeroom for food for the hospital patients. (Those who did not have a companion and were judged by the Nepali staff to be poor were given free food.) The rats quickly discovered the storeroom, and also the way over the top of the wooden partition into my room. For some reason they liked potatoes. One of their favourite pastimes was to bring them over to me, jumping down and running behind the curtain, a Heath Robinson wardrobe I had rigged up. There they would sit and chew the potatoes. I slept under a mosquito net for years, not because of the mosquitoes but to prevent the rats running over my face.

I discovered I was to be the project's business manager. As we were building a hospital on the outskirts of the town, this was quite a task. I am a medical social worker by training, not a business manager, so it was hard for Carl and for me. He gave me two large ledger books. The only place I could spread them out was on the floor. My first job was to tell the staff that we had no money to pay them. The problem was not so much lack of money but the difficulty of getting hold of it.

There were no banks in Nepal then, and so to obtain money it had to be brought by hand from the Mission headquarters in Kathmandu, a journey of two to ten days, depending on the time of year, or from a Gorakhpur bank in India. The latter involved a week's round trip: first the sixteen-mile walk to Butwal, then a bus to the border, the hassle of crossing there and getting another bus to Nautanwa, and the night train to Gorakhpur. Getting the money from Gorakhpur was not the end of the story. It was in Indian currency notes and these had to be exchanged in the Tansen bazaar.

I used to go up the cobbled street by the hospital, with a member of the Nepali staff whom we called Master Jee. At the top of the hill we turned right, past the post office. (Our mail at this time had to come through India; Nepal did not come into the Postal Union until 1959.) After the post office you passed, on your left, the gates into the house of the Governor of Tansen and the surrounding Palpa District. There was a large walled parade ground in front of the house, where the military paraded. The house was a large ramshackle building that houses government offices as well. Inside were long, dusty wooden corridors. There was little furniture but piles of record books and the special Nepali paper made out of tree bark on which 'official business' was written.

The Governor and his wives and family lived upstairs. By western standards they were very scantily furnished and had few facilities. The women folk tended to get bored, as did a lot of the wealthier women in the bazaar. Many later came to the hospital with symptoms brought on mainly by having too little to do.

The Governor's house sided onto the post-office road and also a circle of houses and shops round a central group of buildings, which we nicknamed 'Piccadilly Circus'. Besides cloth and grain shops, there were tailors sitting with their sewing machines at the side of the road. There were very few ready-made garments in those days, so the tailors were necessary— and still are. You could buy your cloth and they would make up anything you wanted.

Opposite the money changers further down the

road were the silversmiths who would make jewellery for you. The money changers sat on the floor and counted out the cash. First they had to look at the exchange rate for Indian currency that day. It changed every day, so a lot of money could be made or lost, depending on when you went to them. We had to watch the exchange rate too and keep two accounts, one in Indian money and the other in Nepali. One problem was that there was no Nepali paper money, so we had to exchange into one or even half rupee coins. These would be counted out in fives, four on the ground and one on top in the middle. I got quite adept at doing this as I had to do it each day with Master Jee. He would come with me to carry the bags of money home.

Ragnar, a Swede, decided that with all the pressures on us, what we most needed was a tennis court. So on the new hospital building site a tennis court was made, and I became, among my other titles, the tennis coach. Besides being tennis coach and business manager, I also tried to improve my language. I helped in out-patients' reception. It was difficult for everyone! The routine might go something like this.

I would say: 'Please give me your hospital card.'

The patient, if an old patient, produced his card, or announced it was lost, in which case our records would have to be searched. It didn't help that everyone seemed to have the same name.

If a new patient came the conversation might run: 'Your name please.' So far so good.

'What is your age?' We usually had a discussion at this point. (There was no birth registration, so birth dates were mostly not known.) However, we usually managed to decide something between us. Where they lived was more difficult; and when I asked their caste I usually got a list of symptoms, and I really couldn't discover why! Other patients who had been through it before usually helped out here. Sometimes I felt close to despair when they said things like, 'I don't understand your talk,' or, 'You will have to speak our language before we can understand you.'

One of the favourite pastimes of the patients while waiting was to search through their neighbour's hair and 'crack' the fleas in it. The level of personal hygiene we encountered was abysmal. But it's no wonder. Water was a scarce commodity in Nepal. I think I first realised the people were really poor when I asked them to wash their babies in hot soapy water. I learned they had no money to buy soap—it was a luxury! Water and the firewood on which to heat it were in short supply too.

I found language learning really difficult. A prayer request sent to my prayer partners stated: 'Mary has no natural gift for language.' This was borne out by my headmistress who had taught me French. She met one of my friends and said, 'Mary will never learn a language.' To encourage me, my friend wrote and told me this after I had failed my second language exam!

So the pressures began to build up. I found being a business manager very difficult; it was hard for Carl too. Years later when someone with proper qualifications came, I said to the new person, 'I have prayed for your arrival since the day I came.' Carl retorted, 'And so have I!'

We had to pass two language exams. When I failed the second one, my Senior Missionary (a force to be reckoned with in those days) said, 'You will never come off probation until you pass.' Our names used to appear on an annual mission report paper, and I had visions of the years stretching ahead and year after year my name appearing, the only perpetual probationer in mission history!

Looking for encouragement and consolation, I wrote to my home vicar, John Page, and told him of my failure in the language exam. He was not a letter writer. He merely wrote: 'Mary, remember God opened the mouth of the ass' (Num 22:28).

The Lord, however, has his own way of comforting. I was taking a Bible class for beginners and feeling very inadequate. One day the women said to me, 'We feel we can talk to you because you are stupid like us and things do not come easily to you as they do to Sister C—! Till then I had been envying her because she was so fluent.

Another time when I was speaking by interpretation, I said, 'Lord, it is no good. I will never learn the language.' Then I heard God say, 'Mary, the girl in the back row will believe.' She did, went away and got married, and came back about eighteen years later and was baptised. I learned that results were not always dependent on my language abilities.

However, life began to be like walking down a long, dark tunnel. There was no way back, nothing to go back to anyway, and no light at the end. God seemed to have abandoned me. I just had to trudge wearily along this long, dark, enclosed tunnel day after day.

Then one day the Senior Missionary announced she was going to Mussoorie in North India, and that I was to go with her. When I got there things seemed even blacker, and I began to feel I was going mad. I pictured myself abandoned in a mental home for the rest of my life, everyone ashamed of me, and no one ever coming to see me.

One Saturday I had really hit rock-bottom. An elderly missionary invited me to go out to tea with her in the only cafe in Mussoorie, Kwality's. She was a very down-to-earth soul, not the sort you pour out your heart to. However, as I sat there things began to brighten up, and I began to feel that maybe I would not have to walk down this dark tunnel for the rest of my life. It was amazing how things began to change after that. I went back and passed my language exam, someone took over most of the business managing, freeing me to do social work, and I had a new experience of God and his everlasting mercy.

Some time subsequent to my 'cafe' experience, I had a letter from my old headmistress, Miss Chester. She wrote: 'I don't know what has been happening to you, but two weeks ago (my rock-bottom Saturday) I felt compelled to go to church and pray all day for you. I hope things are better now.' She had had absolutely no idea what I had been through, but I always feel that to a certain extent I owe my survival in Nepal to Miss Chester's obedience to God that Saturday. I covet similar faithful prayer partners for all overseas workers.

Although we were only a small group, we had a lot of committees. Someone once said of us in the United Mission to Nepal that we were the most 'committeed' group of people he had ever met. We had a Building Committee, Evangelism Committee, Language Committee, Housing Committee, and also a monthly Station meeting to which we all came. These were good, as it gave us an opportunity to meet and air our opinions. As we came from many different backgrounds, our meetings could be very lively, as I discovered at the first Station meeting I ever attended.

We were discussing building the hospital. One person kept changing her mind, sometimes feeling the bigger the better, at other times that we should all be living in mud huts. This happened to be her 'small-is-beautiful week', and as Carl was wanting to discuss more construction, this made for complications. Another couple had obtained their visas because the wife was a nurse. She said now that she had children she could not work in the hospital. Carl felt she had a moral obligation to continue because of the terms of their visa. Feelings began to run high on these and other subjects, with people backing one side or the other.

Then a Swedish missionary, who had been sitting on the floor in the middle of the room, suddenly started to speak in tongues. Although this might be termed 'spiritual input', it didn't solve any problems. It only highlighted another potential source of stress—differences over charismatic gifts, especially as neither she nor anyone else interpreted what she had said (see 1 Cor 14:28).

Afterwards Carl said to me, 'Well, Mary, this is the lot you have got yourself into!' However, it was good for us all to get away from our petty denominational backgrounds and concentrate on essentials. Carl, with his tongue in his cheek, often said that we survived so well because we had no one who majored in theology. Without doubt, a very real love and respect developed among us. We managed to keep a lighter side, as shown in one of the Station-meeting minutes I wrote up. This time we had been discussing the building of a communal laundry.

It was discussed whether everybody's washing should be done all week by one person in one place, by one person in four places, by four people in one place, or by four people in four places. Alternatively by fourteen people in four places, fourteen people in one place, or one person in fourteen places!

Emma felt that one person should wash in one place, while Betty Anne was for four people in one place. Marjory felt only that the washing should be done. By the time the discussion finished, no one was quite sure where their own washing or anyone else's washing would be done, but the unanimous conclusion was that the Station was going down the drain. So it was therefore decided that a communal drain should be built, but whether we should all go down together or separately should be decided later!

Carl felt that if there was a communal washing place everyone should wash together. Others felt that each person was entitled to his or her own tub. Odd Hoftun moved that although the place could be communal, the washing should be separate.

It was felt that it might be difficult for one person to do all the washing, as some people needed more washing than others. Odd then said there would be a separate place for soaking those that were extra dirty, and also a place for clean soaking, washing and rinsing. There would also be a large drain. It was felt that the drain should be large and that it should be ready, if possible, for Carl and Betty Anne's departure.

Then followed a discussion on our living arrangements, always subject to change.

Old House. Concerning the old house, the decision was made that Muna should move into Emma's room, Attan to the Library, Library to the Dispensary, Taksar Clinic to Female Out-patients, Bir Bahadur to Female

Ward, Chukidar to Private Ward, chickens upstairs, someone (but who?) to Anne's room, Manomit to office, Mary to stay put, and all should be cleaned and a lavatory and kitchen built. It was unanimously decided that Ingeborg should be in charge of the horse, horse-boy, garden and large drain.

After an oratorio to bathing and the new drain, the meeting closed with prayer at 10.30 pm.

Poor Ingeborg was to remember the decision about the horse, as it died a week after she started to look after it. It was on the horse-boy's wedding day, and he, poor chap, had to come back to bury it down at the bottom of the garden.

4

Cross-cultural Relationships

Living with people of other nationalities in the United Mission to Nepal was a reason for thanksgiving, but also very stressful. Many of us found adjusting to other nationalities harder than adjusting to the Nepalis. Racial intolerance went beyond colour and language. The attitudes brought about by historical events in our different nations tended to give us more prejudices than we realised. We were all surprised at the tension that arose.

The Nepalis wondered how, with our national histories, we could all live and work together: British, Norwegians, Swedes, Germans, Japanese, Americans, Indians, Swiss, Australians, Canadians and Dutch.

At one period I was Carl's secretary, and I would spell words in the British rather than American way. He would argue that the American way was right and logical, while I thought British was best.

I had a stressful time living with a highly spiritual Swedish missionary who would go off for a day of prayer without warning. She decided to do this the very day the American director of the Mission came to lunch. She was responsible for the catering, but had not made any arrangements, and there were no shops available. I was thankful I had learned to live with such emergencies by keeping a stock of food under my bed. I put together the best meal I could for my two guests. At the end, the American director looked round and said, 'Where are the toothpicks?' Toothpicks my foot, I thought. Who but an American would want one under such circumstances? He should consider himself lucky to have something to pick out of his teeth, without wanting a toothpick as well!

We are told in the Bible that we should give hospitality. Housholds varied considerably as to what they were prepared to do. Before the days of guest houses, we used to put up anyone who came in our only guest room. I remember going out one day and meeting a rather pompous gentleman from the British Council Library who was asking where the nearest hotel was. We said that we supposed we were.

We put him in our only guest room and gave him a tin tub to wash in and told him to throw the water out of the window. He was informed that he would have to vacate the room early the next morning as it was to be used for an all-day prayer meeting. When we later saw his luxurious apartment in Kathmandu, we realised why we had not been considered worthy to receive any books for our local mission library.

Some people really enjoyed entertaining and did not think of any payment. A South Indian man who turned up unexpectedly, however, was very upset to be asked by one family to pay something for his keep. The man, a Christian, felt under the circumstances in which we were living he was 'family'. In South India the custom is to keep your visiting family for nothing, for however long they want to stay.

We were Christians from different denominations. However, we were all in the United Mission, so we agreed not to emphasise our differences but concentrate on building the Nepali church. In the beginning there were so few of us that it hurt when denominational differences arose, as when a Baptist family refused to attend the Christening of a baby of Lutheran parents.

Working and living in a Christian group means that expectations of each other are very high. In the secular world, commendation is sometimes given for 'Christian' behaviour, but this does not happen in Christian circles as it is supposed to be the norm. Of course 'norms' can vary. There is criticism if you fall below your brother's standard. This can cover a wide range of subjects from ordination, candles, attitude to Sunday, alcoholic drink, divorce, the sort of clothes that are permissible, what is considered mean, sensible, generous, etc. The list, sadly, is endless. In the 'world', people are often relieved at our shortcomings; they find it easier to accept one who is 'human' and not super-spiritual.

Playing tennis on Sunday became a source of stress. One of the Swedish missionaries organised tennis parties for the Nepalis on Sundays. This was perfectly acceptable in Sweden, but the English Evangelicals objected; at that time they kept Sunday very strictly as a day for rest and worship. The Scandinavians had candles in worship; again the English objected, as this represented Roman Catholicism to them. These and other matters had to be discussed. The tennis parties were moved to Saturday, but the candles stayed. The Swedish brother became known as our Roman Baptist.

In any community, when communication breaks down the 'no-one-told-me' or 'I-am-the-last-to-know' syndrome rears its head. If you are feeling hurt already, it is easy to build on this impression and convince yourself that you are left out on purpose, or are not part of the 'clique'.

Just such a situation arose when I went to stay some days with a friend in Tansen. She was labelled by the others as 'charismatic'. I had just had a meal with another friend who was 'non-charismatic'. I was asked if I had been told about a prayer meeting that was to take place in the charismatic person's house the next morning. When I said 'no,' my friend replied, 'No, you wouldn't be, it is only for the "in" people. However, you are bound to hear it, for it will take place in the early morning in the room over your bedroom.' I did hear it! I did feel hurt not to be invited. At breakfast the friend with whom I was staying said, 'I am sorry I forgot to invite you to the prayer meeting.' I said, 'Oh, I understood it was only for the "in" people.' 'What rubbish,' my friend said. 'It is for anyone. Some just choose not to come.' However, in any community the 'in'/'out' clique feeling is never far away.

At a party arranged for me when I was going home on leave, I was surprised to learn that communicating seemed to be the most worthwhile thing I had done. One family had remained in the 'old' hospital, while the rest of us moved out to the new. I used to go to see them on my day off. I liked their cookies as well as their company! My chatting about all that was going on had apparently saved them from feeling completely isolated.

Ingaborg used to say, 'If you are feeling lonely, forget yourself and find someone more lonely.' She also said to me (when I reacted about something), 'Mary, you are crucified with Christ. You should have no more reaction than a dead person. If you were really dead it would have no effect on you.' The trouble was, it did!

Another person had a card on her wall with the words: 'I die daily.' But she manifestly didn't; it was the rest of us who had to! She was a fresh-air fiend, and one day Carl wryly said, 'I see she's in the process of killing the rest of us off as well as herself.'

People who are super-spiritual can be really irritating in community life. I had the most wonderful times of prayer I have ever had with Emma, my Swedish tongues-speaking friend, but day-to-day living with her took all the grace of God I had. We are commanded to 'love one another' (Jn 13:34). It is a command, not an option. In any community or relationship, love can grow very thin, and at times needs an act of will. Once, Ingaborg asked me to tell Emma that she was ill and could not go on duty that day. Because they were the only two trained nurses, I treated it as an urgent request. I knocked on her door. Eventually she acknowledged me but refused to open up, and I had to call my message through the door. Later when we met at breakfast, there was an 'at' (atmosphere). I had learned to recognise these. Eventually she said, 'Mary, you should know better than to interrupt me when I am talking to God.' Rather rashly I said, 'Oh, I thought the message was urgent enough to warrant interrupting you, and I am sure God didn't mind.' That flipped it, and off she went into tongues!

I just sat there and gazed at her. Then I began to feel so angry that I could have thrown everything on the table at her. I knew that would not help, so I tried to cool down but she just went on and on. I suppose the problem was that we both felt we had the hot line to God. So, with a deliberate act of will, I turned to

God and said, 'I believe tongues is one of your gifts, but you say that your greatest gift is love (see 1 Cor 13). Please give me your love now and for ever for Emma. I have not got a drop of my own left.' I do not know what I expected, but it was as if God enveloped me, right where I sat, with his love for her. It was never easy to relate to Emma, but I really loved her from then on. One day I asked her how she justified speaking to me and others in tongues without any interpretation of what she was saying (1 Cor 14:5-13). She thought for a moment, and then said, 'Tongues are a witness to the heathen.' I got the message, but I was glad that I had one of the most useful gifts in community living, a sense of humour!

Another aspect of cross-cultural relationships which taxed me was the difference in thinking between East and West. This was described very succinctly for me by a Japanese man whose family lived in the same house as us. The wife would come round asking for help with food, as her husband used to arrive home frequently with unexpected guests—on one occasion with ten men! Admittedly there was no telephone or other means by which he could let her know. Ingaborg and I remonstrated with him. He looked at me rather sadly and said, 'Mary, you westerners have so much to learn about the East. You all go straight at things and sometimes, if you are lucky, hit it, but often you miss it. We Easterners start, as it were, on the outer edge of a circle, and with ever-decreasing circles go round and round the object we want until we have it.'

I knew this from Nepali church meetings. I would sometimes want to scream out, 'Do it this way.' But no, they would talk round and round, seemingly getting nowhere, but on the day it would work. I used to think the Christmas feast would never take place when twenty-four hours beforehand they had not decided which pig to kill. But amazingly the pig curry, rice, leaf plates, helpers and programme were all there—maybe two or three hours after the scheduled time, but in their minds that was the real time anyway.

Following the popular people's movement in early 1990, the king promulgated the new constitution, which came into force in 1991. This declared Nepal to be a multi-party democracy, having the sovereignty of the nation vested in the people, with the king as a constitutional monarch. Previously he had absolute power. There is now a 205-member House of Representatives. Since this happened, there has been an amazing growth in the church. Leaving the church to develop in a Nepali way, with Nepali leadership and no overseas denominational or western bias, appears to have been a good basis for spiritual growth. So I'm thankful that most of the time the Nepalis did it their way, not ours!

Basic sources of conflict are present in the church, whichever nationalities are involved: pride, greed, selfishness, jealousy, sticking to our way of doing things and thinking it is the best, gossip, talking to everyone else except the person concerned, assuming the other person knows what is being said about them when they probably have no idea, or if they do, are very hurt that no one has had the 'guts' to ask or tell them.

I once ran the Sunday school for someone on home leave, fully expecting to hand it back on her return. To my great surprise, when she returned she said she needed time to readjust. This went on for several months; she never indicated to me that she wanted to resume responsibility. The Sunday school was in the old hospital. I lived on the new hospital site. When we had a Station meeting it was raised as an issue that people from the new hospital were continuing to run things in the old hospital. A new rule was made that people in the old hospital should run things there and vice versa.

I was amazed. It then transpired that she had been told that I had said I would miss the children when she came back. In order not to hurt me she had said she did not want to run the Sunday school. But this was not true. We need to be honest with each other in love. Of course I would miss the children, but that didn't mean I was not ready to hand the Sunday school back as arranged. She hurt me much more by not coming to me directly.

Ignoring the principle that we should be open with each other has had dire results in more serious matters of mission policy, resulting in one group or person's viewpoint being heard and not the other. As a result, people bear scars to the end of their lives. These sad results could have been avoided if those responsible for making decisions had discussed the situations fully with all concerned. Otherwise, situations can be blown up out of all proportion. It is good that 'God is in the business of making all things work together for good to them that love Him and are called according to His purpose' (Rom 8:28).

The Bible says: 'If your brother sins against you, go to him [not to others, not to the mission authorities or to other members of the church] and show him his fault. Do it privately. If he listens, you will have won your brother.' Only if he won't listen do you involve others (Mt 18:15-17). How many hurts would be avoided if we did just that. Remember also to say nice things to your brother's face; he may never hear them otherwise.

The devil has lots of 'tools' which he uses continually–and effectively: greed, jealousy, wanting our own way, self-pity, unbelief, doubt, anger, ambition, criticism, fear–which takes many forms. The devil fell out of heaven because of pride (Ezek 28:14-15,17; Is 14:12-13). Pride rears its ugly head in most of us. When I stand back and analyse why I am feeling as I am about a situation, I often find hurt pride at the root.

You probably know the story of the devil auctioning his tools. Someone picked up a small highly-priced tool called 'discouragement'. Why is this so expensive?' he asked.

'Because I can wedge it into anyone, anywhere, anytime,' replied the devil. Discouragement can take many forms: about your own performance, inability to learn a language, lack of seeing spiritual growth, lack of results in any field, feeling overlooked.

Maybe you are not on the latest 'band wagon' and someone is as they have just been on a course about it. New names may be given to things which have been done for years. For instance, the field of Non-formal Education grew out of teaching those who had never been to school. Integrated Rural Development is now bringing together in a co-ordinated way the older fields of water management, agriculture, electrification, community health, education–all to meet the expressed, appropriate needs of each community.

It can and does happen that those doing what may be considered 'old hat' feel themselves second-class citizens. I have known a hospital consultant feel this way because he was not involved in preventive medicine. It is strange that what every Westerner sees as his right–a first-class hospital–can be secondary in the East where the emphasis must, of necessity, be on prevention. But curative and preventive medicine should go hand in hand. This may seem obvious, but it can be grounds for much conflict where the use of staff resources is involved, which can result in one side or the other becoming disheartened.

After some years, mission counsellors were appointed. This meant that now we had people with whom we could discuss problems. It took courage to go to anyone, more for some than for others. Hurts from the past or ingrown attitudes can sometimes make it impossible for us to change and be free. More often than realised, it is a satanic force that is holding someone in bondage, and release is needed in the name of Jesus.

In the East, satanic forces are blatant. Here in the West, I am staggered at the rationalisation and ignorance concerning the influence of spirits. People open themselves up to evil spirits through the New Age movement (much of which is based on Hinduism), Yoga, cults, fortune-telling, ouija boards, tarot cards and devil worship, without even realising what they are doing. The devil is a liar; he is the father of lies (Jn 8:44), yet it seems that the majority of people would rather listen to the prince of liars than to the Prince of Peace (Jn 14:16,27).

We need each other's help. When we become Christians we are called into a family relationship with one another in the Christian church. For some people overseas, doing without the fellowship of their home church is harder than for others. Those who stay and survive become 'bonded' together. Doing without family, or being parted from children and grand-children is a major sacrifice.

On my first journey to India, I had my eyes opened to the intense pain of this sacrifice. Due to a case of appendicitis on board the boat, we had to make an emergency stop at Cape Town instead of Durban. This meant we did not get our mail and had to wait until Karachi, at least a week later. I was disap-pointed, but then I noticed that an older missionary was absolutely devastated that she would have to wait for her children's letters. She went to her cabin weep-ing. Mail service was always a hit-or-miss proposition in Nepal, but usually it created the greatest hardships for those with families. I found I became adjusted to only having mail every two or three weeks, but if a longed-for letter wasn't there, it was hard to have to wait another two or three weeks in the hope that it would be in the next post.

It was interesting to observe the things that people found hard to do without. One family missed bacon so much that they kept pigs. Always high on the food list were chocolate, Marmite and cheese. It was difficult for those at home to realise the cravings we developed. I have more sympathy now for Esau who sold his birthright for a mess of pottage (Gen 25:31-34). There have been many times in Nepal when I would have sold my birthright for a bar of chocolate!

Friends did send precious food items in parcels. However, the parcels did not always arrive. Even worse, one of my bars of chocolate arrived but was half-eaten, with the teeth marks of the customs officer (presumably) still in it. (I suppose he sampled it to test if it was genuine.) Another friend gave a pound box of chocolates to some new people on their way to Nepal to pass on to me. They either thought the chocolates were for them, or that they would spoil in the heat, or that similar chocolates could be bought in India–so they ate them. When they realised what they'd done, all they bought me from India were boiled sweets.

An international speaker from my church once came straight to Kathmandu. My friend had sent me a Yorkie bar, and I was really looking forward to eating it. I met the speaker at the airport. He admitted that my friend had sent him a Yorkie bar to bring to me but he had not brought it as he thought it might spoil in the heat. I would not have minded even if it had been white pulp when it arrived. My fury was quite out of proportion to his action. He took one look at my face and said he would buy me a Yorkie bar when I got back to England. He hasn't. What's more, I don't need one in England–we already have so many sweet things in our diet.

Something most of us had to do without was a hot bath. One national group, the Finns, remedied this wherever they could by building themselves a sauna. Others would rig up a shower with tins and pieces of string. As for me, the struggle to get my tin tub there in one piece was repaid a thousand times. I felt rich beyond measure.

5

Nepal and the Gospel of God

When Nepal opened in 1951, there were no known indigenous Christians. The country had, however, been a subject of prayer for many years. Jonathan Lindell in his book, *Nepal and the Gospel of God*, has named twenty-five missions that worked among Nepalese in India before 1950. In 1935, those who worked near the border formed themselves into the Nepal Border Fellowship. Through this organisation they shared news, information and advice with each other, and encouraged one another to continue in prayer that the land would open. People here and there throughout the world joined with them in prayer. At the Fellowship's annual conferences, they joined the Nepali Christians in singing their song: 'O Lord, hear our prayers, open the door of salvation to the Gurkalis [Nepalis].'

The Nepalis living in India also used to sing a song for the opening of Nepal. One verse speaks of Thapathalli, where the United Mission to Nepal was later to have its headquarters. Another verse mentions Bhadgaon, where the UMN had a hospital. And a third verse mentions Patan, where the UMN built still another hospital. So God wonderfully answered the prayers of those pioneers.

We who came to Nepal found that God had prepared the ground in many places so that we could plant the seed. For instance, one of the Brahmins who owned the hospital house in Tansen was always much more sympathetic and understanding towards us than some of his brothers. Asked why this was so, he told this story. In earlier years, Dr Kitty Harbord, one of the pioneers working on the Indian border in Nautanwa, had been called to Tansen to see his mother, and on leaving she had given her a Gospel. His father, finding it later, was very cross and flung it across the room. Our Brahmin friend, then a small boy, had been curious as to what had so angered his father. So, when his father was not looking, he picked up the book and read it. He was fascinated, and convinced that the story of Jesus was true. He could, of course, never speak of this inner conviction to anyone. He had no contact with Christians until we came, by which time he was a middle-aged man. He realised, however, that we were followers of the One about whom he had read. Sadly he never confessed Christ openly, although he remained helpful and friendly towards us until he died.

Another man had also been influenced by Kitty Harbord's visit. He heard about her from his father, who had been her horse-boy on the journey from Butwal to Tansen, and she had talked to him about Jesus. This man too was sympathetic, and assisted us many times when we had problems with the authorities. He too never openly confessed Jesus, though I know he believed in him. One day when I was reading with him from John's Gospel about people being afraid to witness for fear of the priests, he said, 'Oh, it's just like it is here.' Then, when we were reading John 15, he said with such a light in his face, 'Oh, this is true! It is the living word, and it feeds my heart!'

Dr Lily O'Hanlon and Miss Hilda Steele came to Nautanwa in the 1930s and gradually took over from Kitty Harbord. They formed a band of both Nepali and foreign Christians who worked in the busy dispensaries and went daily to the railway station to distribute literature, sell Gospels, and talk with Nepali travellers. They did the same in the bazaar and at inns and hotels. So in this way the gospel began to penetrate Nepal through the hands, hearts and minds of the Nepalis they contacted.

Dr O'Hanlon and Miss Steele were delighted when the country did at last open. Hilda wrote:

There was a revolution in Nepal which changed the policy of keeping out foreigners. The British Ambassador in Kathmandu was a friend of Dr O'Hanlon and we had an invitation to be the guests of him and his wife in the capital. We could not sleep with excitement before the day came when we set out from Raxaul for Kathmandu. There was a tiny train that carried us up to the foothills—about twenty miles. Then we got on an ancient bus—this was very overcrowded and had mounds of luggage and a few extra passengers on the roof. We were about four-and-a-half to five hours reaching Bhumpedi, the end of the road. There was a Nepali government rest house there, a cook and all we would need of bedding and beds. We had every consideration shown us since we were guests of the British Embassy and the Prime Minister of Nepal had kindly arranged for royal ponies and their syces to be sent down for our use next day.

We had a comfortable night and an early start—in the saddle this part of the journey. How we loved it all, the glimpses of some of the giant peaks radiant in the clear sparkling air of early morning, the green glades we looked up or down on either side—and since we were comfortably settled on the backs of strong, sure-footed ponies, we could give our attention to the beauties of this quite indescribable country of hills and valleys, at that time unspoiled by civilisation and materialism. We got cheery greetings from villagers and travellers and were so thankful we could speak Nepali and reply to their welcome.

The last climb was arduous for even those hardy mountain animals, and their heavy flanks and sweat-soaked coats made me feel selfish to let them carry me. But I had not got my 'hill legs' then, and could not have done the climb on my own feet. At the top was the ambassador and his wife and, greetings over, we proceeded to walk down the miles to where the Embassy car was awaiting us at the end of the piece of road from the city. There was tea and food and then we drove into the city we had dreamed of, talked of, read about and prayed we'd one day reach and see.

A happy, thrilling and very helpful fortnight followed, when we met the prime minister and other ministers and government officials. We asked permission to trek over land to Pokhara in the west and so out to Nautanwa by the route from there. We were informed His Majesty the King was graciously allowing us to occupy two seats in the royal plane, which was taking a government party to Pokhara on 12 March, and that was 1952. His Excellency the British Ambassador accompanied us and we had a trusty Christian Nepali whose birthplace was Pokhara. What a flight that was—I needed eyes to watch the grandeur of those magnificent mountains to the north; I wanted another pair to gaze down on the hills, valleys, rivers, forests and villages below us, and all the time the lump in my throat got bigger. God had not let me down, he had brought me in. The plane, after a few hours in Pokhara, returned to Kathmandu, taking our friend the ambassador and the other people in high places with them. We two were in the heart of Nepal in a village where no white women had ever been—and we were no longer 'important' to anyone but him who had taken us there.

We walked, explored, asked innumerable questions and lived for three days in the guestroom of Buddhisagar, our Nepali friend's house. We had sent in a petition to His Majesty the King of Nepal for permission to open medical work in Pokhara, and had a refusal. But we were encouraged by the Minister for Health to make another application after we had visited Pokhara and seen the possibilities and the need.

One of the features of that fifteen-mile long valley in those days were the wonderful trees, many of them sacred—Papal, Bask, Swami, Banyan. There were great tall cork trees, red with blossom, and cotton trees. And there were grassy plateaux with herds of goats and buffaloes grazing and some horses too. There was the long, two-mile single street with attractive stalls of Tibetan goods, carpets, saddle mats, baskets, food of the Nepali type, like corn and sweet potatoes, tobacco, cheap cigarettes, unglazed pottery. Best of all there were friendly people, not a few who had been down the long track to us in Nautanwa for medical help, and many more who knew us by hearsay. We talked and soon learned we were both welcomed and needed in Pokhara, and there were promises of help when we needed it.

On the fourth day we took the track to the south. We walked about four miles to the end of the valley, and then began the climb. There were no 'flat bits', it just went up and up—rugged, rooted with trees, in places shale—but always up, and where it was not very steep it was more than very steep. I reckon it was about three miles, and we were both pretty breathless as we sat on the rim of the valley once again, quite silenced by those massive giants that dominate the valley when the light is bright, and seem mysterious and remote, almost threatening when the clouds mass and the sky is lowering.

Pokhara valley is 2,600 feet above sea level; over it the Annapurna peaks tower to heights of 26,000 feet and more. From that rim there is a fantastic panorama; you look at the great mountains and you look into the gorges and valleys between.

That night we spent in a Nepali home, ex-patients of ours from Pokhara. The second day we climbed down into a valley called 'the Field of Butterflies'. There was a clear, broad river running through it, and we kept seeing birds and butterflies and fish that were all new to us; our progress was rather slow. We decided on a meal, and while Buddhisagar cooked on a picnic fire, I went to get sticks and Dr O'Hanlon sat on a grassy bank near a high rock. I heard Buddhi scream and looked round. Above Lily were a group of monkeys who objected to a white face—or so it seemed. They were chattering as to who should push the first rock over onto the head of the objectionable foreigner, who was quite oblivious of their presence above her. Buddhi's yell caused enough consternation to give the intended victim time to move to safety!

That night we were at the end of the valley, and also at the foot of a second climb, not so long or steep as the first. We were doing short climbs and drops along ridges all that day, and then settled in a pilgrim's hut the last night—just a mud-and-plaster, two-storey building with a thatched roof and a notched treetrunk by which to get from the downstairs floor where you cooked on a camp fire, up to the loft in which we slept on the floor in our sleeping bags. There is no furniture or kit in these places and they are usually flea-infested and very dirty. Also, as the floor is not plastered, all the smoke from the cooking fires goes up and the occupants of the upstairs room are kippered! Next morning, we tackled the two climbs; first the 'little rise', then down again to a valley and so up the 'big rise', which brought us out on the Tansen ridge. We spent a night there; it is quite a big, prosperous town. March 8 we got back to Nautanwa, and promptly sent in another request to the Nepal government for permission to start work in Pokhara.

There was a good deal of correspondence, but at last, in the first week of November 1952, with visas to reside and work in Nepal, we set out. Two lady doctors, three nursing sisters, five Nepali colleagues, and myself. We were on the way, at last, to live in our land of hills and valleys.

It took them six days to walk to Pokhara, and there they started medical work and a mission known today as the International Nepal Fellowship.

In Tansen, under the United Mission to Nepal, Carl and Betty Anne Friedericks went to Tansen in 1954. They soon began to lay the foundations for Christian worship. They arranged for a small hymn book to be printed in Tansen bazaar, with hymns written by Nepalis for their own people. This was good, as it meant that from the beginning we avoided having only hymns that were translations from English ones; there were some, but they were never the most popular, the Nepalis preferring those in their own style of music. Producing a hymnal was also a brave step: it is against the law in Nepal to engage in any form of proselytisation. Any Nepali changing his or her religion was liable to a year's jail sentence. And anyone responsible for another's conversion could be given a six-year sentence.

Nepal interprets 'freedom of religion' as everyone being free to follow the faith into which they were born–to follow the traditions of one's forefathers is how it is put officially. Nepal is a Hindu state, with the King regarded by many as the incarnation of Vishnu, one of the three main Hindu gods. Thus politics and religion are closely bound together in Nepal. Indeed, in its effort to preserve stability in the country, the government desires that its citizens adhere to Hindu traditions.

On the staff in Tansen were Nepali Christians, who had Indian citizenship since they came from the Darjeeling area, but when I arrived in 1957 there were not yet any baptised indigenous Nepali Christians.

As we foreigners were allowed to 'follow the traditions of our forefathers', we felt this included our meeting together for worship each Sunday. In 1958 I wrote: 'We have been encouraged by the Nepali service. We have had a variety of people attending, including outcastes, workmen from the hospital building site, a Buddhist, a Hindu holy woman, and a high caste Newar woman who had amazingly walked over a mile to come.'

Because we were Christians, Ragnar felt it right to start work on the building site with prayers each day. I wrote: 'It is wonderful to hear three or four workmen praying in the name of Jesus. Recently, when there was no one to take the service, they carried on on their own and read the Bible and prayed. We have also started having prayers in the ward each day. We ask the patients first if they would like us to, and we always get an affirmative answer. You would have to be a very strict ward sister not to be thrilled to see people sitting on the ward floor and beds listening to the Bible, which of course most have not heard before. People have come specially in time for the ward service, and they listen with great interest. I take Gospel Recording records on the wards each Sunday.'

Betty Anne also started a 'Sunday school' (held on Saturdays, as that was the school holiday). When she was away, I took over as superintendent. This meant helping the Nepalis with preparation of the talks each week—and I could use no English! I gathered the children by means of the Gospel Recording records (no cassettes in those days) and at the end gave out foreign stamps to those who had learned the Bible verse each week. The children were mostly boys, and numbers fluctuated for no apparent reason from about sixteen to sixty.

We were not troubled by the law forbidding us to 'proselytise', the official interpretation of this being 'not to force anyone to change their religion'. Christianity is not a matter of adhering to a set of religious principles, but rather a free-choice relationship with Jesus Christ. We knew we could not force anyone to become a Christian, and believed that all conversions were the work of the Holy Spirit in the heart. No one can *make* someone else love God.

In knowing Jesus, we had found the 'pearl of great price' (Mt 13:46), and wanted others to hear about him and to have the opportunity to know him for themselves.

Open-air meetings and door-to-door evangelism were out. I wrote: 'We cannot preach directly, but in the slack periods of Out-patients I have been reading *The Stories of Jesus* in Nepali to myself for the exam, and quite often someone comes and reads it over my shoulder.' I found, too, when reading on a bus, for example, that I could pass the book on—a good way to speed the good news. Literature in Nepali was in such short supply that people were eager to have any books they could get.

We also put up a book rack in the hospital from which patients could take books. We collected English books, since there was a great eagerness to learn English, all higher education being in English. We ran a lending library each day, and this gave us contact with students. I was pleased to find that teachings from the Sermon on the Mount (Mt 5–7) were included in some college exams. Realising it was from the Bible, some students came to me for further enlightenment.

The Nepalis at first considered all Westerners to be Christians, as it was the 'religion of our forefathers'. Most of them learned fast that this was not so, when tourists, hippies, mountaineers and trekkers invaded their land.

In the beginning we were regarded as outcastes (and still are in some places) and people would not drink tea with us or take water from us. One of the main reasons for this was that we were cow eaters, and the cow is sacred in the Hindu religion.

In Hinduism there are many gods, and most Hindus are quite prepared to add Jesus Christ to the list and to accept him as being a way to heaven. Where we parted company was when we pointed out that the Bible claims Jesus Christ as the only way. Jesus said, 'I am the way, the truth and the life; no man comes to the Father but by me' (Jn 14:6). 'Neither is there salvation in any other, for there is none other name under heaven given among men whereby we must be saved' (Acts 4:12).

It takes a lot of courage and faith for a Nepali to become a Christian, to step outside one's culture and follow an unfamiliar religion. However, God has his own way of revealing himself. Nepalis have visions and dreams about God and Jesus much more than people in the West. We were once reading about the angel coming to Mary in the Christmas story, and I said to my Bible class, 'Have any of you seen an angel or had a vision of God?' To my amazement, practically every one of them had. These were illiterate women who mostly could not read or write, but their hearts were hungry for God and open to him. He communicated with them in a way they understood. Unlike us in the West, they could also see evil spirits. You never had to convince Nepalis that evil spirits existed.

Carl had made the decision that he could not begin medical work until he had help and could reasonably handle the patients. Since he was not able to get sufficient assistance from outside Nepal, he at once began to prepare such assistants as he needed, selecting and training young Nepali men and women in simple nursing procedures, laboratory work, treatment of patients and use of medicines.

Among the trainees was a woman named Oma Shanti, who from the beginning had shown an interest in Christianity and attended the services and Bible classes. After a time she accepted Jesus as her Saviour, and expressed a desire to be baptised.

Another trainee, Bir Bahadur, came from East Nepal. He had first become interested in Christianity by reading a tract called 'Way of Salvation', which had been given to a friend who rejected it. Bir Bahadur read it. Talking about it much later, after he had changed his name to Timothy, he said, 'It seemed to bring a warm glow round my heart.' Several years were to pass before he had another contact with Christianity, when God sent an intrepid border missionary, Mildred Ballard, to work in his area.

Mildred was in need of a mail runner, and Bir Bahadur got the job. Mildred wanted to start medical work. She saw the potential in Bir Bahadur and decided to send him to Carl for training. The flame lit in his heart by the tract was nurtured by Mildred. He came to Tansen and joined the fellowship there, and it wasn't long before he too became a Christian.

We had no pastor, and a male nurse from Darjeeling was running the services. Oma Shanti and Bir Bahadur were both asking for baptism, so we decided to ask Pastor David from Pokhara to come over and take the service. It was carried out quietly in a nearby stream. We missionaries were told by mission headquarters not to attend. The UMN leadership felt if any missionary had been found at the site of a baptism, there was a danger that the whole mission could be kicked out of the country for 'converting' Nepalis. It was made more difficult for Pastor David to understand, as in Pokhara, where he lived, the International Nepal Fellowship missionaries always went to the baptism of Nepali Christians.

I was the only one living in the house from which they left for the baptism. They could not understand why I was not going with them. Pastor David said to me, he thought we would go and stand with them as fellow believers, as they did in Pokhara. 'Are you afraid?' he asked me. He was visibly upset and disappointed. In vain I tried to explain that it was biblical to obey the authority under which one worked (1 Pet 5:3). As I stood and watched them go, my eyes filled with tears. Later one of the missionaries, realising how upset I was, read to me Zechariah 13:6–'And one shall say unto her: "What are these wounds in your hands?" Then she shall answer: "Those with which I was wounded in the house of my friends." ' These words were so apt I have never forgotten them. It was the first but not the last time I was to find the Nepalis completely mystified by our policies relating to them.

It was, however, a day of rejoicing. The first seed of the church had been sown. After this, others showed greater interest, and we began to feel we were in need of someone to head up the church work.

A Christian pastor from Butwal, named Prem Pradhan, visited us in Tansen and expressed a desire to come and work in the hills. We prayed and discussed whether to ask him to come as our pastor. It was against the law for Nepalis to change their religion; what might happen to him and to us if we invited him to come?

Prem Pradhan was a high-caste Nepali who had been brought up in India in a Hindu home. His caste mainly consisted of businessmen, and he had been trained for a successful business career. One day, passing through the bazaar in Darjeeling where he lived, he paused to listen to an open-air preacher named Bakht Singh. Bakht was a very spiritual man and a skilled communicator, and he caught Prem's attention. Prem listened spellbound and then, against his will, found himself drawn again and again to hear this man's words.

At last there came a day when he was convinced by Bakht Singh's message. He realised that Christ had died for the sins of the whole world, and that included him. His wealthy parents were horrified that their son should abandon his high-caste Hindu background to join the low-caste, cow-eating Christians. He was disgracing them. There was no alternative so far as they were concerned but to turn him out.

Prem joined the church Bakht Singh had formed in India, and became an itinerant preacher for them. Later he pastored a church in the Assam hills. However, when Nepal opened in 1952, he had a great desire to go to his own land and tell his people the spiritual truth they had been so long denied. So he came to the border town of Butwal. We decided to take the risk and ask him to come to be our pastor. After he came, things moved fast and many people began to ask for baptism. Prem was eager for them all to be baptised.

We held a church committee meeting at which Ragnar and I were the mission representatives. At one point, I remember, feelings ran high. Prem was for baptising everyone who asked for baptism. Those who had been around Tansen longer were for caution.

There followed a fierce argument on the scriptural role of baptism, the amount of knowledge, teaching and experience people needed before being baptised. The Philippian jailer (Acts 16:33) and the Ethiopian eunuch (Acts 8:36-38) were cited as examples, who, as far as is known, had very little knowledge before they were baptised.

The meeting had come to a complete deadlock when suddenly, in a most amazing way, the Holy Spirit seemed to come upon us and take over. Things which a few minutes before had been big issues simply melted away.

Tension mounted in the next few weeks as up to about sixteen people asked for baptism. Prem felt some were not ready, and he said so. We prayed that only those who would be able to stand persecution would be baptised. He invited all to attend preparation classes. One decided he would wait until later; others realised they had not fully understood all that was involved.

In the end eight went off secretly in the morning with Prem Pradhan to the river for the service. Again, we were not allowed to go. One man, who had been very brave and definite about his faith felt, when he actually got to the river, that he could not go through with the ceremony. He never was baptised and eventually left the church. Seven people were baptised. It was lovely to see their faith and zeal. After this it seemed as if nothing would hold back Prem and the baptised believers from proclaiming the Christian faith to anyone who would listen in Tansen.

6

Persecution Comes to Tansen

Such exciting things were happening in Tansen that we began to feel as if we were living in the days of the book of Acts. Our mere presence in Tansen was beginning to cause the townfolk to question certain aspects of their own lives. The Hindu leaders had always outwardly received great respect from the people: it was customary for people to bow down and kiss the feet of the leaders when they met them, but this was happening less and less. The people saw that we did not do it.

We had been given land on the outskirts of the town on which to build a hospital, and this we began to do. It had been given to us because it was the place where the carcasses of dead animals were thrown, and no one dared walk there. We, of course, did not realise this until later, when told by the local people. They said, 'We could never go over the land where the hospital is built because of the fear of the spirits of dead animals that roamed there. Since you came, we are not afraid, because the Spirit that is with you is greater than the other spirits, and they now cannot hurt us.'

There was a trained Nepali pharmacist in the town and he disliked us. Before we came he had a complete monopoly on drugs. There were many stories of what he had been able to get away with before we came, such as charging 100 rupees (about £5 in those days— an enormous sum for a Nepali) for a dose of castor oil to cure constipation! Carl tried to co-operate with him and let him supply drugs on prescription from the hospital, but he refused. In fact, he took every opportunity he could to work against us.

At the crucifixion of Jesus, Pilate and Herod became friends, when before they had been enemies. So, as certain factions in the town began to have their self-interests affected, they had meetings together to discuss how to get rid of us.

After the service of dedication for the new hospital site there was a shower of rain which prompted one of the Nepalis to remark: 'God is blessing your hospital; when we build a new building we have to get the Brahmins to come and spit on it, but God is doing it for you!' Remarks like this did not, of course, endear us to the Brahmins.

We had to bring water for the hospital from the town. Because the hospital was for the benefit of the local people, we were surprised when the people rioted against us for taking the water. We were to learn over the years that water was an extremely emotive issue. Carl, however, with the help of members of the Nepali staff, managed to get reason and order to prevail, and we were allowed to take the water we needed. Those who were against us met with the governor for further discussion.

One Sunday afternoon Carl received a letter from the police asking for the names of all those who had been baptised and those who had baptised them. I remember going to the church to ask what we should do. The Christians all agreed it was an official order which must be obeyed and told us to give their names; as you can imagine, we felt dreadful. We met and prayed and waited to see what would happen.

After a few days those named were all called to the police station. The pastor and two others were away, but the other seven went. They were questioned for an hour and a half about their faith and about who had forced them to become Christians.

Before they went we discussed the promises given in Luke 21:12-15 where it says: 'They shall lay hands on you, deliver you up to the synagogues and into prison, bring you before kings and rulers for my name's sake. It shall turn out to you for a testimony. Settle it therefore in your hearts not to meditate before what you shall answer, for I will give you a mouth and wisdom which your adversaries may not be able to gainsay or resist.'

The police hoped that the Nepali believers would implicate the missionaries and thus give tangible evidence that we had been proselytising. We would then face the prospect of having our visas rescinded and being sent out of the country, which did, in fact, happen later to some missionaries. We wept when we learned that the Christians had met together before going to the police station and agreed they would not mention us.

Six of them stood up boldly to the questioning and said they were Christians but that no man had made them Christians. They themselves had realised that God had come into this world in the person of Jesus Christ and had been crucified on the cross, not only for the sins of the whole world but for their own sins. He was risen from the dead and was alive today. It was Jesus who had come into their lives and changed them.

One of them, an illiterate woman, was asked if we paid her husband who worked on the building site. They hoped to show that we had given him money to become a Christian. She said, 'Yes, they pay him, and they would pay you too if you worked for them!'

Another couple, given a cup of tea, bowed their heads in prayer before they drank. The police said, 'We gave you the tea to see if you would pray first. Now we know you are real Christians.' It made me wonder how many Christians in England would pass that test. Surprisingly, the police were not unsympathetic to them; one of the policemen turned out to be a Christian from Darjeeling.

At the end of the day, the magistrate called them all together and said that if they insisted on saying they were Christians he would have no alternative but to sentence them, according to the law of Nepal, to one year's imprisonment for changing their religion. He said he understood they wanted to be Christians, but advised them to say in court that they were Hindus. They could continue to believe in Christ in their hearts, but they should outwardly perform the Hindu ceremonies. He urged them to consider their decision and instructed them to report back the next day.

The magistrate was effectively suggesting that they continue to believe in Christ with their hearts, but to deny him with their mouths. As they went to their homes for the night, one of the verses their leader gave them to ponder was, 'Whoever will deny me before men, him will I deny before my Father in heaven, and whosoever will confess me before men, him will I confess before my Father in heaven' (Mt 10:32-33).

The next morning they returned to the court. They were asked in turn if they were Christian or Hindu, and if they intended to remain as baptised Christians or go back to the traditions of their forefathers. One by one they stood before the magistrate and declared their faith in Christ. One of them, when sentenced to a year in prison, said, 'I would be glad to go to jail for twelve years for the peace Jesus has given in my heart!'

We Westerners were not allowed to go to the court but later we heard them coming down the hill by the hospital. They were on their way to the jail. They were singing hymns and walking with their heads held high in the midst of their captors. One woman was pregnant, one had a little girl of two months in her arms, and another was accompanied by her three-year-old son. The crowds who had gathered to see them go threw taunting remarks.

They were taken to the town jail, a grim-looking building with a high wall on which a sentry paraded. The men and women were separated: the men were in a room with ten others, and the women with five others. The prison had mud floors with only straw mats to sleep on, and as it was cold and damp we asked to be allowed to take in blankets; this we were able to do. We were also permitted to take food, but it had first to be inspected by the guards. There were large iron-barred gates through which we could talk to the prisoners.

The seventh Christian who had gone to the police station denied his faith when first questioned, but later repented and asked to be put in jail with the others. However, this was not allowed. The pastor and the other two who had been away at the time knew that if they did not come back but went instead to India, they would probably never be imprisoned. However, they still decided to return. They reported to the police, were tried for their faith, and put in jail with the others.

At first the believers were very active, using their Bibles to talk to other inmates and also singing hymns. However, after a short while their Bibles and hymnbooks were confiscated. Here we were, outside the jail, while our Nepali brothers and sisters were inside. The tension we experienced mounted from day to day. Although it was a half-hour walk to the jail, one or more of us visited every day.

We experienced tensions among ourselves, too, some feeling we should try to get legal help, others that we should simply pray and rely on God to secure their release. We felt increasingly 'bonded together' as we were conscious of the opposition in the town against us.

The numbers at church services and Sunday school dropped off, and some who had been friendly to us ceased to be so. Others showed their faithfulness in befriending us. We found the local people divided; some felt that although they themselves had no wish to be Christians they saw no reason why others should not be free to be so if they wished. One Hindu friend offered what I felt was an astute comment: 'If they had taken the trouble to read the history of the Christian church they would have left you alone to fight among yourselves over petty issues. Persecution will only make you grow.' How true his words turned out to be.

One team member felt so strongly about legal aid that he managed to get a Kathmandu lawyer to take an interest in their case, a brave thing to do in those days. This lawyer has remained a good friend over the years. However, he was not able to secure their quick release. The cost to the team member and his family was that they lost their visas and had to leave the country. Though they remain active for the land of Nepal, they never returned to work there.

It was a very harrowing experience to visit the jail, especially since prisoners were often taken out to be beaten. The guards used to tell us to go away, as it was not a sight suitable for us to see. After five months I wrote: 'I'm afraid there is little hope of the prisoners being released. In fact, in the last two weeks things have become worse rather than better. Under extreme pressure four of them have denied their faith, hoping for a quicker release.' Shortly after, two of the four repented of this act, declaring they really were true Christians.

We felt that God had given us a promise that they would not break rank (Joel 2:7). We found it a real trial of our own faith. It was so easy to look at circumstances and not at God, especially when those inside got downhearted, which so often happened. The jail was dirty and very infested with insects and rodents. We obtained permission to spray it with DDT powder. God encouraged our spirits by the fact that the day the 'spraying party' went in was the day after the Christian who was pregnant had had her baby in the night. A sister who was with the party was able to examine mother and baby and found everything to be fine. This was the only time we were allowed in the jail. It was a special comfort to the mother, as her first baby had been born with spina bifida and had died after a few months.

Our hopes for an early release were raised several times. On one occasion a four-man committee sent by the King came to look into cases in the jail. We expected that they would do something about 'our' prisoners. However, it became obvious they were not sympathetic towards them, and to make it worse they made open remarks about us. They said that we had 'bought' those in the jail, that we were foreign spies, that we were serving up sugar-coated poison in the shape of hospitals and libraries. They sought advice from people in the town whom we knew to be most opposed to us. It seemed as if Satan was openly triumphing. Yet again and again, as we turned to the word of God, we gained assurances that this was not the case. The words given were: 'The triumphing of the wicked is short...Thou shalt bruise his head...The wicked plotteth against the just and gnasheth upon him with his teeth. The Lord shall laugh at Him for He seeth his day coming...The God of peace shall bruise Satan under your feet shortly' (Ps 37:13; Jn 20:5; Rom 16:20).

The pastor said that a month in jail was equal to a whole year in a Bible school for training in the Christian life! They certainly had their trials. All the children got measles. One night the women's side got flooded out when there was heavy rain. All the floors were mud, so even when the water subsided they were left wet and not easy to walk on. It was very damp for sleeping too, as all their bedding and the straw mats they slept on had got soaked. The smell and the creepy crawlies increased as well. As it was the rainy season, it rained every day, and getting anything dry was difficult for them. We managed to get some sawdust in to help dry things off, but we were not allowed to take anything else; the restrictions were very tight.

We did, though, have encouragements. On the King's birthday thirty-one prisoners were released, but sadly none of ours. A man came to the hospital asking for a Bible, a hymn book and a copy of *The Pilgrim's Progress*. He was one of the released prisoners, and because of contact with our friends, he wanted to go on reading.

The Christians were still in prison when the time came for my home leave. I went down to say goodbye, and they all crowded to the barred gates. I said how bad I felt at going home and leaving them in jail. They said, 'Sister, you must not worry.' (Over the years Nepalis were to say this to me many times.) 'You go home in the will of God and we'll stay here in the will of God.' The pastor then said, 'Let us commend Sister Mary to the Lord.' And there, with those inside bowing their heads and I outside, he prayed for me and for those to whom I was going, thanking God for their prayers and support. The guard made me move back a little but otherwise did not interfere. At the end of the prayer we said goodbye, and with a heavy heart I continued on my way down the trail to go home.

We attempted to take steps to get the prisoners tried. There had been no official trial, so they had not been sentenced and it was impossible to find out how long they were expected to be in jail. However, shortly after I got home, news came that their case was to be tried in Kathmandu in two months, in September. Then in November came the news that eight Christians and their children had been released. One was kept three days longer than the others, as he had to serve a full year's sentence for having given rice to his elder son after becoming a Christian (thus making the son unclean in Hindu eyes).

These eight were released after a summary judgement given by two judges in the Nepal Supreme Court in Kathmandu. They lost their inheritance, or partition right, in the joint family system and were declared Hindu again. This latter item in the judgement had no basis in law—just the judges' own idea.

The pastor was not released. He was sentenced to six years' imprisonment—five years left to serve. He and his wife seemed prepared for him to stay on alone. Friends in Tansen wrote that it was a refreshing experience to go and see him; he was allowed outside the jail to see visitors. He felt that through his being there much prayer would be made for him and for Nepal. He wrote, 'Inside the jail the Lord gives me the privilege of being a living witness. Nowadays there are many political prisoners here. They are studying the Bible with me. They, too, desire religious freedom.' The lawyer prepared a petition for a Royal Amnesty for him, but nothing happened.

Year after year he went on witnessing for Christ in the jail. He wrote: 'The authorities in this place thought that by putting us in jail they would quench our joy in Christ and stop our Christian activities, but the opposite has happened. This action against us has drawn us nearer to Christ, and we feel his presence more real than before. Our persecutions cannot hinder our fellowship with Jesus. Praise God! The anger of men and iron bars cannot make our spirit captive. "Surely the wrath of man shall praise Thee" (Ps 76:10). History shows that persecution of Christians always works out for the furtherance of God's kingdom among men. Therefore we understand that our imprisonment has a divine purpose. Maybe the case against us will lead to full freedom of religion in Nepal.'

In 1991, after an uprising, Nepal is now working towards becoming a democratic state. Christmas Day 1991 was a public holiday for the first time. One of the church's Christmas services was shown on television to illustrate how Christians celebrate Christmas. From all over the country comes news of people accepting Jesus Christ as their Saviour. People are being added to the church daily (Acts 2:47). There is still not complete religious freedom; Nepal is still a Hindu state, and it is on the statute book that you cannot change your religion. However, things have come a long way since Prem and his friends were put in prison.

Prem was moved from Tansen to Kathmandu but still not released. Then, suddenly, after four-and-a-half years, he was given a royal pardon. It may be that the desire of an American mission doctor, who was advising the King on his heart condition, had an influence on this decision. The King had asked the doctor if he could do anything for him. He had replied: 'Yes, release the imprisoned Christian pastor.' So it happened that he was freed with a year-and-a-half of his sentence still to run.

7

Social Work

It was not easy to go back to Nepal again in 1962. I had become used to the comforts of the West, the ease of having to speak only English, of seeing and being with my friends. I thought how much better off, materially, they would always be than me. I asked God to give me a promise for my return. At a service in Torquay, Isaiah 55:12-13 was read. I was just thinking it seemed too good a promise for me when the minister said, 'Take a promise for yourself out of this passage.' So I did. The promise was: 'You shall go out with joy and be led forth with peace.'

We went by boat to Bombay. In my daily reading for 11 November (the day I left) was the passage: 'He led them on safely.... Behold I send an angel before you to keep you in the way.' For the train journey from Bombay to Nepal, which lasted two days and a night, and for the night on the trail—when I shared a room with six men, two women, a child, a dog, some chickens, lots of bugs and my porter—it was good to have an angel too!

On the way up I stopped at the jail to see Pastor Prem Pradhan; he had been deprived of his Bible for three months. I couldn't get closer to him than fifteen yards. He was, of course, behind the bars of the jail. I was glad to find that he was in good heart and was counting it a privilege to suffer for Christ.

Only three of the others who had been in jail were still in Tansen. Two had gone to work near Kathmandu, while the remaining three were at Bible college in India. A young Nepali male nurse with some Bible training was leading the church, together with three Nepali deacons.

Carl greeted me, saying, 'I hope you have enjoyed the trip out! As there was a war between China and India, it looked as if we might have to leave any moment. Since Nepal was inbetween the two warring countries, we thought we might be invaded by the Chinese. We had an escape route planned, and an emergency pack of clothes, drugs and food ready in case we had to go quickly.'

Carl, who had stayed on in China when the communists took over, had said, 'If I say you are to leave, you go! I want no self-styled martyrs here.' He was right, we did have at least one potential martyr among us.

However, as things remained calm for some weeks after my return, Carl felt it would be good for me to do a social survey. Hilda Steele had moved out of Pokhara to start a new work in a remote area—a forty-eight-mile walk from Tansen. It was decided I should go to her area to do the survey. As I was leaving, Carl said, 'If you see Chou-en-lai (the Chinese prime minister) coming over the hill, don't wait to try to convert him. Just run here as hard as you can.' Happily, no Chinese appeared; the social survey was done in peace. It turned out to be an enjoyable project.

Carl wanted more social work input into the hospital. A South Indian Christian girl, Annamma Verghese, had come to work in Nepal. She was interested in learning social work, so I started to train her in a two-year programme. We worked together in the hospital two or three days a week, and went visiting on two or three other days. We discovered a lot of social needs and problems among the patients.

When I first went to Nepal, I saw the Nepalis as cheerful, industrious, courageous and trustworthy people, outwardly happy and apparently free from many of the difficulties and problems that we face in the West. However, the more I entered their lives and learned about the problems in their homes, the more I realised that basically their lives and needs were little different from ours. The lonely, the dissatisfied, the perplexed, the fearful and the needy are met with everywhere in the world.

There was the woman from a wealthy bazaar family who was always coming to the hospital with seemingly little wrong with her. Outwardly she looked happy and prosperous. The doctor, however, referred her to us. In the course of conversation she told us that she was the second of three wives in a household with forty-two members. She was childless and felt rejected. She could not read and had little to satisfy her.

A girl with tuberculosis of the spine was faced with a year of inactivity in a plaster spinal jacket. All her daily activities of cooking, cleaning and carrying water were stopped. She could not read, and in those days there were very few radios and no television. We were able to bring new interest into their lives by teaching them to read Nepali and to knit.

A poor widow came to the hospital and was found to have inoperable cancer. Her home was not far away, so we were able to visit her. She became a Christian before she died, and her son is now a church leader.

We found it essential to follow up patients being treated for tuberculosis. Many who started treatment did not finish it. We grouped the patients into visitation areas, and plotted the location of those who had defaulted on their treatment. As they were widely scattered it was only possible to visit two or three houses a day.

We found that as soon as there was an improvement in their condition, patients stopped coming for treatment. Later we devised a scheme by which patients could pay a 'down payment' for two years' treatment; but they still defaulted. Understandably, when the hospital is several days' walk away, the immediate takes priority over the distant. Some years later at a conference in Kathmandu, I was asked to speak on the reasons for people defaulting on TB treatment. Among other things, I mentioned that they could not leave their buffaloes. Buffaloes tend to be 'one-person' animals and allow only that person to milk them. (When we kept buffaloes we often resorted to the subterfuge of dressing someone up in the usual milker's clothes, hoping the buffalo wouldn't look round and notice the difference. It didn't always work!) To replace a buffalo was an expensive business. One of our vets said that a buffalo was of more value in Nepal than a wife, since a wife could be replaced at no cost!

At the end of the conference, a friend came up to me and said, 'We took your point about the buffaloes, Mary, and have decided to build a line of buffalo sheds at the new Patan Hospital so that patients can bring their animals with them to hospital.'

Annamma and I once visited a patient a two-hour walk from the Tansen hospital. She had been put in a body cast for TB of the spine. When we got there the patient was sitting alone, crying, in a dark one-roomed mud hut. We stayed a while and talked with her. Because she was so depressed, we decided to visit her again the following week. However, when we got to her house, there was no sign of the patient. Then we heard a shout from the fields, and there she was, standing and cutting the heads off the millet and throwing them into a basket on her back. She looked a different woman and was perfectly fit. We enquired what had happened. She explained that she had become so fed up with the body cast that she had got someone to cut it off. Then a neighbour told her that the cure for her illness was to eat 'chipli kira'. These were large green slug-like creatures which people swallowed whole to cure themselves of all sorts of diseases. Just the thought of it is enough to make one sick! However, the chipli kira had done the trick in this case. Or could it have been misdiagnosis? I went back to the hospital and told the doctor he was wasting his time; to cure his patients he should go out and collect a supply of chipli kira. He didn't take me seriously: professional pride, no doubt.

Besides TB follow-up, we also helped with leprosy rehabilitation. There was a government leprosarium a three-hour walk from Tansen, and we took turns going in twos each month. When we first went, people on the road said, 'Why are you going to help those whom the gods have cursed; you will bring the wrath of God on yourselves.' The patients had no medical treatment until we came; they had been sent there so others would not get the disease. Many were disfigured, without noses, fingers or toes. They had been rejected by their families; they felt the gods had cursed them. Some had disease-free children with them. One of the children rescued at that time later came to Christ and became a hospital nursing superintendent.

The news spread that we had medicine to cure leprosy, and patients began walking over the hills to our mission hospital. Many of them had been turned out of their homes and lived in caves in the hillside. Their relatives would bring them food, but leave it some distance away so they themselves would not catch the disease. They had not been touched by another person for many years, and wept when we did so. A man arrived, having walked ten days, and said: 'Where is the God who can cure leprosy? I hear he is here.'

I remember one leprosy patient well. She was typical of many patients, but more fortunate than most. She came one day with her brother-in-law to the outpatients' department, having walked three days. The doctor diagnosed her condition as an early case of tuberculoid leprosy, which was not contagious. The doctor, Annamma and I explained to the patient and her relative that there was no danger that others would catch the disease and her condition could be cured, but that she must come for regular treatment. She and her relative appeared to understand and they went home. You can imagine our sorrow when a week later she turned up again in a very upset state, having been turned out by her husband. We decided she should go for a period to the leprosarium in Pokhara, which was run by the Nepal Evangelistic Band. We felt, however, that an effort should also be made to get her back home.

It was suggested that I make a home visit—a bit

different from one in England! I was not able to get full particulars of the journey, but I knew the name of the village, the headman, the husband's and the sister's name. I set off with a Christian Nepali named Daniel as my porter, and we walked eighteen miles the first day. The road was a dirt track which led over several mountains. We had no sooner walked down a steep path to the river than we would be climbing up again. People we met assured us that we should reach our destination by the next day. There are no marked paths in Nepal, so we had to ask our way from anyone we met. We were given accommodation in the home of some Nepalis that night. The people were very hospitable and gave us a meal of rice and curry, and we slept on straw mats using the bedding we had carried. Nepalis do not charge you for staying in their homes, but you usually pay for anything you eat or drink.

We got up early the next morning and walked until we came to a village called Wangla. The schoolmaster there was very helpful, gave us a meal, and directed us on our way to the next village. Again we went down to the bottom of a valley and then high up the other side, arriving in the village by evening. We had to stop early, because the people said we should not travel the road ahead at dusk, as it went through a jungle. So we stayed the night in the village on top of the hill, with superb views of the Annapurna range. The children there had never seen a white person before.

Next morning we went down, down, down, only to go up, up, up. I felt I was going to the top of the world and thus was not surprised to find the name of the village was 'Star'. The two cups of tea I managed to find there were about the best I have ever tasted. Then we met some people from the village we were looking for. They said there was no one there by the husband's name, and we wanted another village fourteen miles further on. Not far in a car, but a long way on your feet.

So up, up we went again. The scenery was beautiful, with snow-capped mountains rising in the background. But most of the time on treacherous mountain paths, you worry about where to put your foot next, not the view. After the ups there are always the downs. Down, down, then up again. It was approaching nightfall and we were trudging up a winding path through the forest, no sign of houses anywhere. I said to Daniel, 'Hadn't we better start looking for somewhere to stay?' He seemed unconcerned.

To my relief we came out into a clearing in the forest–surely there had to be some houses here. Well, there was a large wooden construction in the middle of the clearing, but it didn't look inhabited. We walked over to look at it and peered in. Inside was a large pit. 'What is it?' I asked. Daniel's answer was nonchalant considering the circumstances: 'A tiger trap.'

I looked around. There was no indication which way to go to find somewhere inhabited. After praying for guidance, we decided to take one of the paths going on up through the forest. I thought it unlikely that anyone would be living on top of the mountain, but still it did look the best path to take.

I was quite irritated with Daniel, because he seemed completely unconcerned. Where was my trust in God? Hadn't he promised to take care of us? When people get righteous, I tend to get unrighteous and want to hit them! Nepalis remain remarkably serene under such circumstances. They have a 'whatever will be will be' philosophy of life. This is one of the reasons they make such excellent soldiers; the Gurkha regiments are famous throughout the world for their courage.

My strength, courage, and serenity were fast ebbing away when we came out on top of the mountain. There was a clearing, and in it a small circle of houses. We found one family of forty-two people living there, only two of whom had ever seen a white person before. With the usual wonderful Nepali hospitality, they offered accommodation for the night and a meal of rice and vegetable curry. I was so tired I fell asleep while they were preparing the meal. I woke to find myself surrounded by the entire family, all sitting up to watch the unique sight of a white woman eating. Daniel was telling them about Jesus.

We spent the night on straw mats on the mud floor of one of their houses, and made an early start the next morning. This is never difficult, as all village Nepalis get up early to collect water from the spring, cut grass for their animals, and husk the day's rice.

The family gave us directions to the village we wanted, which was only four or five hours away. We arrived at 10 am, found the house, and asked to see the patient's husband. He was out in the fields and, to our amazement, refused to come in to talk to us. Daniel went out to try to persuade him, but without success. So I went with Daniel and we talked to him in the middle of the field. We explained the position regarding his wife, that she did not have a contagious form of leprosy, and that she wanted to come home to him and her two children. He absolutely refused to have her back, and said that he had taken two more wives. Neither would he let her have access to her children.

He was totally unco-operative, and gave us no refreshment or hospitality, though the rest of the family were sympathetic. We had no alternative but to turn round and walk back to Tansen, though by a more direct route. The trip had taken us six days and ended in apparent failure.

So what to do now for our rejected patient? It did not seem right for her to go on living in the leprosarium when she did not need that sort of treatment, but where was she to go? It was then that we learned our visit had not been as fruitless as it had first appeared. The rest of the family were furious with the husband and his lack of hospitality to us a disgrace in Nepali eyes. Over the years the patient and her relatives would apologise for it again and again. Now they were moved to help the patient. One of the relatives got her a house in Tansen and helped her to start a cafe there. They also arranged for her children to join her and go to school in Tansen. The husband was willing, as he had other children by his new wives.

Even though she was entirely free of infection, such was the fear of leprosy in Nepal that if people had realised she had had the disease, no one would have come to her cafe. Her little finger was slightly bent, and the doctor was afraid this might give her away. He decided to admit her to the hospital and straighten it out, but what to do with the children, then aged eight and ten? She was a stranger in Tansen, so none of the neighbours would take them. Annamma and I decided to run the cafe and look after the children while she was in hospital. Thus she would have no loss of income.

We learned to make 'Sal Roti', a type of doughnut made by forming circles of batter in hot fat. Since we were Christians, most people were afraid to eat food cooked by us for fear of being ritually contaminated. So we did not do a very good trade. However, we and the children enjoyed the 'doughnuts' we made. It was a success in that the patient came back with a normal little finger and was able to run the cafe for many years afterwards.

As you will have gathered, to visit any patient it was necessary to walk. Sometimes, however, we just walked round the Tansen bazaar visiting patients. We were usually offered refreshment, most frequently a cup of tea and a soft fried egg. The latter was served on a small tin or brass plate, sometimes with a teaspoon but as often as not with no utensil. It's not easy to do a social investigation and at the same time try to eat a soft fried egg with your fingers. If you don't believe me, you try it on your next outing.

One hot May day after visiting many homes, Annamma and I had eaten our fill of fried eggs and I was threatening to go home if we were offered another. Also, since there were no toilets available, the number of cups of tea one consumed in a day could become a problem. Even after years in Nepal, I was never comfortable just squatting anywhere.

Our next call that day was to a more rural home. Sure enough, out came the tea and the fried egg. We didn't know the people well enough to say, 'Please don't give us anything to eat or drink,' because they might be embarrassed if they had not been thinking of doing so. I was wondering what to do with my fried egg. I had large pockets with plastic bags in them for such emergencies, but a soft fried egg is not the best thing to have in one's pocket.

Our hostess left us momentarily, and just then a goat appeared. Now I was brought up on children's tales that goats eat everything, so its arrival seemed a God-sent opportunity to get rid of my fried egg. With a deft sleight of hand I gave it to him. Imagine my horror a few moments later when, on the return of our hostess, the goat spat the egg out at her feet! So much for relying on children's stories.

My very first home visit in Nepal was with Dr Marjory Foyle, who asked me to accompany her to a maternity case. When we got there we were surprised to find the patient was a goat! Nonetheless, she was safely delivered, I holding her head and Marjory handling the other end. Mother and baby did well.

A visit I always remembered was to the husband of a diabetic patient about two days' walk away. She always came to hospital in a bad state. On enquiry we found that her husband would not believe she was ill, since she did not have any obvious symptoms like worms, diarrhoea, cough or fever which he could identify. He therefore thought she was lazy and beat her. We sent messages asking him to come to see us, but with fields and animals to look after it was not easy for him to get away. So over hill, over dale I went to see him. He listened, seemed to take in what I said, and promised to let his wife come for treatment. He kept his word. The wife was delighted, and said her husband never beat her again.

We had to care for a number of abandoned children, or those who for one reason or another had no home. I could tell many stories, but for me the most dramatic was Tek's story.

I was running the library in the old hospital and, as usual, a lot of children had piled in, as they did every day after school. I knew them well, and they usually chatted about all sorts of things. Today they said, 'Tek has come for you to look after him.' I did not really pay much attention, thinking it was one of their jokes. However, at the end of the time, Tek was still there. I shut the library and, suggesting he go home, I went upstairs. However, I was not very happy and went down again, to find Tek curled up on the verandah like a kitten. He was about seven. I woke him up and asked him to tell me his story.

He said he had been in prison with his father and had seen me visiting 'our' folk there. He and his father had been discharged from jail and, as they had no home, the police had put them with a family who had been willing to employ his father as a goatsherd. His father, however, had stolen the goats, sold them and disappeared with the money, probably to east Nepal. Tek's mother was dead.

The family naturally didn't want to keep Tek, so they took him back to the police. Since then he had been with several families, none of whom wanted him. So he had taken to wandering around the bazaar, living off his quick wits. In the bazaar he had seen me again and decided that since I was a friend of his friends in jail, I must be a kindly soul who would help him. At this point two of my Nepali friends came in, so I asked them to have Tek for that night and give him a meal. This they did.

The next morning Annamma and I took Tek to the police station. They said, 'Yes, what he said was quite true, and you can have him if you want him.'

I replied, 'If I have him, he will be brought up as a Christian.'

'That's all right,' said the police.

What to do now? I have often thought about it afterwards. I suppose if I had been longing for a child I would have felt that God had given me one. As it was, I have a 'thing' about single white women bringing up national children, and had signed a mission form to say I would not do so. I did wonder if, like Amy Carmichael, God was calling me to start an orphanage or children's home, but that did not feel right either.

I asked around my Nepali friends whether any of them felt they could bring Tek up as their child if I paid for his upkeep. I knew that this had been done with great success before. To my great sorrow no one responded to this. I got in touch with various orphanages and drew blanks all round. In the meantime, he stayed with Nepali families.

As I was coming back from India to Nepal, I told my friends, who ran a girls' home on the border, about him. I knew they could not have him, but was glad of their prayer help. To my surprise, shortly after my return to Tansen, I got a letter from these friends saying their pastor felt he should have Tek in his own family. Tek went off and settled happily with them. When he went to school, he came first in his class in Scripture, and second overall. He became a Christian, and worked for a time with Operation Mobilisation. He is now married and living in India.

As we visited among the inpatients and out-patients, all sorts of social needs became apparent. When nothing could be done medically, these patients were referred to us. It was helpful for the relatives to be able to talk over the prognosis and learn ways of making the last days of the patient's life as comfortable as possible. Carl told me not to worry, since the Nepalis themselves would know of pain-relieving herbal plants, and I found this was true. There were, of course, no nearby social agencies, but the local village councils knew their own people and on occasion could be helpful.

One day a high-caste Brahmin came to the outpatient department with his daughter, a dear little doll of a child aged two. When the doctor went to examine her, the Brahmin said, 'I have come to give her to you. Her mother had a mental breakdown and has run away, and I have "killed my love" for this child (a Nepali expression which means just that). Please take her.'

The doctor sent for me, and together with the Nepalis and the father we talked over the whole situation. The Nepalis were unwilling for us to take the child, as they felt that thereafter anyone else who didn't want to take responsibility for their children would then come and dump them on us. So the father and the little girl were sent away and told to bring a letter from the village council (panchyat) saying it was best for the child to be given to us. Weeks went by and we heard nothing, so a letter was written to the panchyat asking what had happened. Again, weeks of silence. Then one day the panchyat leader arrived with the little girl, Radha, and her brother Komal, aged four. The father had run off and left them both.

This time we admitted the children to hospital and asked the panchyat leader to obtain a letter giving us permission to have the children. Weeks passed and, in spite of our writing, nothing happened. Meantime, the children were endearing themselves to everyone.

The little boy was bright and intelligent and very solicitous of his little sister, feeding her and making sure she got a share of whatever he had. Then their mother turned up. There followed days of agony while we wondered if she would take the children. But she did not come again, and there was no further news from the village.

So Annamma and I decided to go out and visit. Everyone in the village was of the opinion that the parents would never take responsibility for the children, but would always be going off and leaving them. The father came back, and with the help of the panchyat the children were signed over to us.

My friends over the border took them into their children's home. When I went to see them the little boy was sitting in the church with his hands folded, praying. Both children were happily adopted by a childless Christian couple.

8

Journeys

Community social demands were made on our hospital. One day a Brahmin lady came in to say that the whole of her village, a few hours' walk away, had been struck down with cholera. She described graphically how no one was able to work, and it sounded as if they were dying like flies. Carl decided we should respond. The trouble was that the hospital was very busy, and no doctors or nurses could be spared to go.

So I was sent. I went with a brand-new medical student who had just arrived from America and, of course, did not speak any Nepali.

We set off down the hill across the valley to a village on the other side, about a four-hour trip, as the lady had said. A Nepali porter came along to carry medicines, water-purifying kits, and our bedding, since it sounded as if we would need to stay there several days.

As we descended into the valley, the American began to moan. In the valley rice was planted and we had to wade across fields with no clearly marked path. The mountain views were superb, but my companion was in no mood to enjoy them, especially as we were told that the village was on the other side of the mountain!

We crossed the mountain and eventually reached the top of the next, only to have our destination pointed out to us on the summit of the next range. So down and up again. In Nepal it's common for people to shorten the time they tell you it takes to get to their village, because they fear that if they told you the truth you wouldn't go.

It was toward evening when we arrived at the village. I was puzzled, as there appeared to be no signs of the distress or devastation described to us. No one came out to say how glad they were we had come. However, since it was a very scattered village, we thought maybe the problems were in another part. We were taken to the home of our informant, and I asked where the cholera patients were. Her husband replied, 'Oh, there aren't any. I just wanted you to see my mother who lives on the other hill.' Needless to say, the American couldn't believe it when I translated what he had said.

By this time, of course, we were surrounded by a crowd of interested onlookers. Some of them did look ill, and as it was a long walk to the hospital–which we knew–and since we had brought medicines with us, we examined many of them. We did not, however, climb up and down another mountain in order to visit our host's mother!

There was no alternative but to stay the night with our host. He refused to let us into his house. In his eyes we were Christian cow-eaters, we were thus unclean. Instead, we slept on mats on the open verandah. In the middle of the night it started to rain; the wind blew the rain in on us in sheets.

I was angry by now, and unclean or not, I hammered on the door of the house, and knocked and called until the owner got up. I then told him what I thought of him and his hospitality (I've been told I'm very fluent in Nepali when angry). I told him what an awful ambassador he was for his country, and what did he think this student doctor, straight from America, would tell his friends when he got back home?

The rain was still pouring down, so after listening to my tirade he reluctantly let us into the house. However, he absolutely refused to admit our Nepali porter who was a lower caste. However much I pleaded, the poor chap had to spend the night outside.

In the morning our host asked us if we would like some eggs. I thought this strange since Brahmins do not eat eggs. However, thinking we might as well get something out of the trip, I said, yes, we would. He then said, 'They are half a rupee each' (the going rate at that time). Our porter exploded, and I learned a lot of new Nepali words! He kept up a flow in this tone all the way back to Tansen.

The American, not finding any tea shops and insisting on boiling and filtering his water, collapsed on the last hill. I had to leave him in a house and send someone down with fresh water and refreshments before he could make it back. Later, when he was asked to go on another village trip, he said, 'They will have to bring four dead bodies to the doorway of the hospital before I move out of this place to go to another village.'

Carl, who was given to jokes, used to ring me up on the hospital internal phone from time to time to ask me to go to a village down with typhoid, smallpox or cholera. My reply was always, 'You go, I'll stay and run the hospital.'

Annamma and I once went on a trip to try to bring home a leprosy patient who was in the government leprosarium. She was seventeen and had been there for four years. She had been turned out of her home because of deformed hands. The doctor had now operated on them: they looked normal and she was free of infection. The doctor felt she should return to her village, but the village people did not want her. So, taking her with us, we went to persuade them that there was no reason why she should not live at home.

We spent a noisy first night sleeping in a house with twelve men. One blew a whistle, another played a drum, and the others sang while we were waiting for our meal of rice and vegetable curry. In the midst of their singing, the rice pot began to leak, so the men took it off the fire. We had to give them the pot we were carrying with us, or we would have had no supper.

We had had quite a job organising our load for the trip. Our porter had told us he would carry only sixty pounds, so we tried to keep it down to that. We had to take bedding, medicine, books and food, in case we could not get any on the way (hence the rice pot). At first the load was eighty pounds, so we took off some rice. We eventually reduced it to seventy pounds, which he ended up carrying quite happily.

We had brought a tape recorder, so after they had sung for a while we offered to play them some of our songs. But this met with little response. They preferred making their own music. They sang until long after midnight, and we were unable to sleep until they stopped.

It took us four-and-a-half days to get to the patient's home, the last part being a three-and-a-half-hour climb up a mountain above the town of Baglung. It was a beautiful location; the village was etched against the Himalayan snow-line. The patient was well received by her people, and we left an official 'freedom from infection' certificate with the headman. We hoped this would signal the beginning of a breakdown of prejudice against leprosy patients.

At every home we stayed in, there were opportunities to talk about Christ. One night, when we were waiting for our evening meal, we heard incantations of Hindu worship coming from the house. (We were in a small bamboo hut adjacent to it.) Later, when we went into the house for our food, there were about twelve men gathered. They said that every night now for a month they had gathered together each evening to read the Hindu scriptures. This led on to talk about 'our' Scriptures. After supper we went back to our room, and some of the men followed. We asked if they would like to listen to the tape recorder. After listening they all took a booklet called *Way of Salvation*. Three people bought John's Gospel, and the man of the house a New Testament. He had recently returned from visiting many Hindu shrines in an attempt to find peace.

We'd like to be able to say that the leprosy patient settled happily back in the village, but we had not done our 'homework' well enough. We did not realise that she had left her heart behind in the leprosarium. So, after a period in her village, she walked back to the young man she loved there. He had such bad leprosy he could not be rehabilitated outside. I lost touch with them, but I hope they were happy. There was a sense that the leprosarium was the only security she had ever known.

A journey that Annamma and I really enjoyed was to the home of Jaisora, a TB patient who lived in

Gulmi district, a good day's walk from Tansen. She first came to hospital because of her TB Because she was ill, her husband had turned her out and taken another wife. She had their two children with her. She had got to know the leprosy patient who ran the cafe. She also tried to run a tea shop to earn her living. Jaisora came to church several times and seemed interested in spiritual things.

Annamma was taking a group to a yearly Bible school held in Pokhara, three days' walk from Tansen. She invited Jaisora to come too and in an amazing way she arrived in time. Nepalis in the villages have little means of knowing dates, and we'd had no news of Jaisora. Both Annamma and I felt that it was right for her to go, but there was no way of knowing whether she was planning to do so.

Imagine our joy when, the day before they were due to leave for the conference, Jaisora turned up with her two children. I'll always remember her wide-eyed wonder that we had doubted she would come. Where was our faith? She almost seemed to rebuke us, wordlessly saying, 'Isn't he in charge of all things?' I must say it felt very much as if he was, and we just had the privilege of being swept along in it.

A party of six set off the next day on the three-day trek to Pokhara. All of them were eager and expectant, none (except Annamma) having ever been to anything like it before. Due to the poor communications, it is always difficult to organise anything for hill Nepalis. You never really know how many will turn up. Nepalis, however, are very adaptable, and when several hundred arrived, the Ramghat Church was turned into a dormitory at night, as well as being the meeting place during the day. Cooking was done on open fires outside. Chapattis, curry and rice were the main food. Apart from a plate, no utensils were needed as everyone ate with their hands. The Nepalis used to tease me when they saw how much crockery I needed, and the amount of washing-up I made when I entertained.

God blessed the conference and somehow kept it hidden from the authorities. I went to help Hilda Steele, while Pavitri went with some others from the area to the conference. Pavitri brought the Tansen group back via Pyersingh (where Hilda lived). They were a very excited, joyful party, who arrived having done the one-and-a-half-day trek from Pokhara. We were soon hearing their stories.

It seems that we in the west delight in making faith as complicated and intellectual as possible. So it was thrilling and encouraging for Hilda and me to hear the simple testimonies of how the group had met the living Lord Jesus in Pokhara.

Jaisora had a dream. Jesus came and stood beside her and said, 'Jaisora, I died for you on the cross; for you my hands and feet were pierced.' Then he said to her, 'It is finished' (she couldn't have known that was what Jesus said when he died on the cross) and told her to go back to sleep. As she slept, she realised for the first time that it really was for her that Jesus had suffered and died. It was so real to her that Jesus became her living companion, day by day, from then on.

The next day I went with them on the forty-eight-mile trek to Tansen. Jaisora then went the extra day's walk to her home. She immediately began to tell her neighbours what had happened in Pokhara. When she contracted TB her husband left her; he was now living with another woman in the village.

Her father and mother-in-law owned the house
she lived in, and were much more sympathetic to her
and her two children than they were to their own son.
They allowed her to go on living in the house, which
was a wonderful provision, and instead of being the
abandoned wife, she was very much supported by her
in-laws. This she attributed to God's goodness and
mercy to her.

When we went to Jaisora's house, the local people
always gathered to hear about Jesus. Her next-door
neighbours became believers. Jaisora was always
spiritually hungry. The Nepali church practises
tithing (the giving of the first of either income or
produce to God for his work). In Pyersingh and
Paimey, people used to bring offerings of millet,
maize and rice to the church. I always found it very
moving to see their generous giving out of their pov-
erty. God is, however, no man's debtor, and when this
principle is adhered to, God blesses.

Jaisora was a generous giver. If she had had a box
of alabaster ointment, she would have broken it over
Jesus' feet, like Mary. She used to talk about what she
could give to her 'beloved Jesus'.

One time she had a great desire to bring us some
fish, which we could not obtain in Tansen. However,
there was none in the village; no one seemed to have
caught any. Then, on the evening before she was leaving home, she heard a knock on her door, and there
stood a man with fish for sale. When she joyfully
brought it to us, and told us the story, she added, 'So I
said "thank you" to my beloved Jesus.' We did too, as
fish was one of the things we really missed.

One Christmas she brought her son and daughter,
and told us that living conditions had improved even

more. Her husband had died, and the woman he lived with had immediately gone off with another man. This meant that Jaisora and her children had inherited everything and did not have to share it with the other woman. She and I were delighted that Christmas.

Sadly, although she kept up her TB treatment regularly, she had begun late, and her condition gradually deteriorated. Unknown to me, she had asked God that she would die in Tansen Hospital, and that I would be there. By that time I had moved out of Tansen, but on one of my infrequent visits I was told, on arrival, that Jaisora had been admitted. I went at once to the ward. It was obvious that she was not going to be with us much longer. She herself knew it, and her delight at seeing me sealed for her the joy of going to be with her beloved Jesus, who had answered her prayer. She died shortly afterwards. Although she would be very surprised, I always think of Jaisora as one of the great little women of faith and prayer.

9

The Mountain Begins to Move

God was beginning to show that maybe he had other plans for me. I had done a social survey in Pyersingh where Hilda Steele lived. Hilda had always been interested in village work, and when others took over her work in Pokhara, she asked Pastor David, the church leader there, where he thought she should go. He said, 'I think you should try to get work in the village of Pyersingh. There are two women there, Pavitri and Channi, who have recently been converted, and others who are interested. I feel you should go to strengthen their faith and teach them.'

This seemed an impossible thing to suggest. To work there Hilda would need a visa. Pyersingh was in West No. 4 district, and there was no mission work in that area. However, Hilda felt that God could be in this suggestion of Pastor David's.

She had no encouragement from anyone; rather the reverse. Everyone felt, and said, that it was impossible that she could ever get a visa to go and work on her own in a new area. However, Hilda was a very determined person, and so she felt she should apply for a visa and see what would happen.

She flew to Kathmandu and went to Singha Durbar, the main government building. With much prayer and some trepidation, she started to walk up the long marble steps in front of the building. As she slowly went up the steps, trying to compose in her mind what she was going to say on her visa application, she was joined by a Nepali man. Hilda never had any idea who he was. However, he recognised Hilda and gave her a friendly greeting. After asking after her health, he enquired if she was still interested in working in the villages of Nepal! Hilda then explained that she was at that moment on her way to try to get a visa to work in the villages of West No. 4 district.

They went on up the stairs, talking together, until they reached the floor where Hilda would have to make her application. The Nepali turned, Hilda thought, to say goodbye, but to her surprise he asked for her passport. He took it, and to her amazement went with her into the office, walked over to the young woman sitting at the desk, and said, 'Please make out a visa for Miss Steele to work in West No. 4 district.' He then bowed to Hilda and walked out; she never saw him again. To Hilda, it was as if an angel had intervened. For without his help, she almost certainly would not have obtained her visa.

The woman looked up at a dumbstruck Hilda and said, 'It will take a little time to process your visa, Miss Steele. Will you please come back tomorrow and I'll have it ready for you.' Next day the young woman handed Hilda her passport, and in it was written permission to allow Hilda to live and work anywhere in West No. 4 district. The woman then asked Hilda to sign for her visa. One space was for 'occupation'. Hilda said later, 'I always like to be sure things are of God, so I wrote "Missionary".' Owing to the law in Nepal against conversion, no one was allowed in on a missionary visa. The woman, however, looked at what Hilda had written, smiled, and said, 'So you are a missionary, are you?'

'Yes,' said Hilda. 'I would not be here if I wasn't.'

So with her new visa for West No. 4 in hand, Hilda came out of the offices in a state of wonder and thanksgiving. But now what to do? One step was over; the next step was to get permission to work in Pyersingh—and that would be even more difficult.

She first went to the governor of the area in his office in Syanja. She could not come right out and say that she wanted to go to Pyersingh, because the governor would surely ask, 'Why there?' And then what would she say? She couldn't give her real reason for going to Pyersingh—which was to follow up converts. Therefore she merely offered to help somewhere in the district, and asked the governor where he would like her to go. She was an agriculturalist by training. The governor suggested she go to a village called Kuin, which was a three-hour walk from Pyersingh.

So to Kuin she went, and met the headman there. As she had had medical experience with Dr Lily O'Hanlon, and had also done a missionary medicine course in addition to her agricultural training, she offered them medical help. For this they were very grateful, as there was no medical help in the area apart from the witch doctors. The nearest hospital was in Pokhara, two days' walk away.

The headman was not able to give Hilda very adequate living quarters. For a time she lived on a raised platform under a thatched roof, such as travellers shelter in at night. The platform was reached by going up a notched log. There was no privacy, and she often woke early in the morning to find patients crouching beside her bed. At that time her bed was only a straw mat spread out on the platform with her sleeping bag on it. But Hilda didn't mind. She was just happy to be there.

One of the first things Hilda did was to go to Pyersingh to find Pavitri. Channi was still a patient in the leprosarium in Pokhara. She couldn't find Pavitri. Everyone seemed secretive. Then she heard a small boy say, 'She is ill.' His elders tried to shut him up, but Hilda had heard and was determined to find out where Pavitri was.

The villagers were reluctant to tell her, but after much questioning, she found out that Pavitri was at her mother's village of Paimey about two hours' walk from Pyersingh and Kuin. So off Hilda went to Pavitri's mother's home, only to find she was not there. Again folk hesitated to say where she was. In the end Pavitri's older brother told Hilda that Pavitri was down in a lower village, staying with her sister. He offered to take her down to her.

Hilda went with him and found Pavitri very ill indeed. Her sister and brother-in-law were very anxious about her, as Pavitri had refused to let them get the witch doctor. As this was the only medical help they knew, they were distressed that she wouldn't let them call for him. Pavitri told them she had become a Christian. She said that she no longer believed in witch doctors, but in the living God. If he wanted her to live, he would send someone to help her.

Hilda, of course, had no idea of the spiritual battle that was being waged in that small mud house, or the significance of it for the future of the church in that area. She stooped and entered the door of the small, dark, thatched cottage. With her eyes adjusted to the thin beam of light coming through a slit in the wall, Hilda saw an emaciated Pavitri lying on a straw mat by the fire. Her sister was crouching by, feeding firewood into the hollowed-out mud under a tripod, on which stood a kettle.

Pavitri hardly had strength to move, but her eyes lit up when she saw Hilda. She was very weak, and burst into tears. Hilda saw at once that Pavitri was extremely ill, and that curing her was going to be a hard struggle, not only with the disease (Hilda had no idea what was wrong with her) but also with the evil spirits that pervaded the place. Hilda realised that she was too sick to be carried over the bumpy, dangerous road on the two-day journey to the hospital. She would have had to be carried on a man's back in a basket, or in a hammock slung from a pole and carried by two or more men.

As this was out of the question, Hilda knew it was up to her to do what she could. It was a long uphill battle in more senses than one. Hilda went up and down each day from Kuin to treat her—four hours' walk a day over very difficult paths. Many times she thought she was going to lose Pavitri. Hilda's hands were strengthened by the prayers and support of the church in Pokhara. Pastor David, hearing Pavitri was ill, sent out one of the Nepali deacons, Philip, to see if there was anything they could do to help. Hilda and Philip had been on many treks together in the past.

To Hilda's great relief Pavitri gradually began to improve and gain strength. Pavitri's sister and brother-in-law watched, thinking perhaps they should have called the witch doctor anyway. What did this foreigner know about how to deal with the spirits that had made Pavitri ill? If she died, they feared they might bring down the wrath of their gods on them-selves. After all, they were childless, so it would not do to anger the gods further! However, their respect for Hilda, Philip and Pavitri held them, and they did not call the witch doctor.

Pavitri continued to improve. Hilda learned later that this was a great blow to the relatives of Pavitri's husband, for it was they who had caused her illness. They had given her poison, hoping to show what could happen to people who became Christians!

Back in Kuin, life continued for Hilda under dif-ficult conditions. Limited communication, limited supplies, poor accommodation, and opposition from the Hindu leaders were some of the problems taxing her at this time. I remember her telling me that she was so low in cash and supplies that she prayed for a patient to come so she could sell some medicine and earn half a rupee to buy an egg to eat! It is never easy to start a new work.

Just as Hilda was beginning to wonder what she was going to do, the governor of Syanja came on an official visit to Kuin. He had decided to visit her. He was so horrified at the lack of facilities the village had given her that he did the unprecedented thing of beat-ing up the chief Brahmin with his shoe! This was the greatest insult he could have given him. He then said that as they had treated her so badly he would not let her stay there.

He knew there was an empty school building in a village about two hours' walk from Kuin. He thought she could go and live there, and he was sure the local people would be glad to have her help to start a dis-pensary. Imagine Hilda's delight when she heard that the village was Pyersingh! She needed no second bidding to go. She moved into the upper floor of the school building, and opened a small dispensary downstairs.

After she had been there a few months, Pavitri turned up. (It had been her husband's village.) She announced that she was coming to live with Hilda and look after her. After some demurring on Hilda's part, Pavitri went off and came back with a bundle of firewood under one arm and a live chicken under the other! She then told Hilda where the fire was to be and reorganised their accommodation.

Pavitri had been through quite a lot before she came to be with Hilda. Her father had been in the Gurkha army with the British in the First World War. He had been badly injured in France and invalided home on a full disability pension. This had made them one of the wealthiest families in the village. Her parents had twelve children, six of them surviving. Pavitri had an older brother and sister, and two younger sisters and a brother. Her father died when her younger brother was two. After his death the family was much poorer.

As was the custom, her mother was keen to get her daughters married off as quickly as possible. So when she had a good offer for her second daughter, Pavitri, arranged by relatives in Pyersingh, she accepted it without even seeing the man or knowing much about him.

The first Pavitri knew about it was when a group of her relatives arrived to take her to the man. She was about fifteen. She refused to go. They and her mother insisted that she must go. The family would lose face if she did not go, a very serious thing in those days. She resisted as much as she could, clinging to the posts of

the verandah where she was sitting, kicking and biting to try to fight off her relatives. What, however,
could a fifteen-year-old girl do against all her relatives
and against her mother, who had given permission for
the marriage. In the end they took her by force, carrying her protesting all the way up to Pyersingh to a
man who was at least thirty years her senior and who
had another wife living with him.

Years later, when Pavitri and I were talking to
Amma (Pavitri's mother) about it, Amma said, 'What
else could I do? I needed to get my daughters married.'
She said she had not been told that the man already
had a wife and was at least thirty years older than
Pavitri. Amma had not met her own husband before
she married, so she had accepted that that was how
things were done. I don't think we ever convinced her
there was much advantage in seeing one's husband
beforehand anyway!

Over the years I found that many Nepali women
were rather cynical about marriage. A lot of them told
me that if they had had the chance they would have
remained single as I was, and so would not have to be
involved in sexual relationships.

Pavitri's husband worked in India. He left the
other wife at home and took Pavitri with him to Bombay. They were there for a few years when, to her great
relief, he died, leaving her a childless widow of nineteen. But her troubles were by no means over.

She went to his work office to collect the money
due to him. The cashier came and asked her to sign a
form, which she did. He went away to get the money
but later came back to say they were sorry, they did
not have sufficient cash to pay her, and would she
come back tomorrow. When she did return the next

day, she was shown the form she had signed the previous day saying she had received the money!

There was nothing she could do—a defenceless Nepali widow in a foreign country, miles away from home. It was then that she had her first contact with Christianity. A Sikh who had become a Christian offered her a job as a nanny to his children. She accepted, and travelled with this family to many parts of India. They eventually took her to Delhi and gave her enough money to get back to Nepal.

When she got home three things happened. She was made to do the last Hindu rites for her husband all over again, even though she had done them in Bombay. This angered her. Second, the other wife insisted that she divide everything with her, even to tearing her saris in half! The third thing was that her very close friend, Rhoda, had got leprosy and become a Christian in the leprosarium in Pokhara. Rhoda was so enthusiastic about her new Christian faith that she wanted all her relatives and friends in Pyersingh to hear about it. So she invited two of the Christian leaders, Pastor David and Daud, to come and take what were really evangelistic meetings in Pyersingh. A brave thing for all of them to do, knowing, as they did, that they were going against the law of the land.

Softened already by the kindness of the Sikh Christian family in India, disillusioned by the treatment she had received from the Hindus since she came home, Pavitri's heart felt drawn to what she had heard of Christ from the Pokhara Christians. Because her husband's relatives were unkind to her and were continually threatening her, she asked permission of the local village council to go to Pokhara and look for work.

A Gurkha officer proposed marriage and offered to take her to Hong Kong, but she refused him. She got permission from the council to go to Pokhara, so off she went. A missionary family befriended her there, and she became a nanny to their children. They taught her to read and write, and while in Pokhara she became a Christian and was baptised.

Later she felt she should go back home and share her new-found faith, but her mother turned her out and the local community publicly excommunicated her. And, as we know, her husband's family tried to poison her. She was very lonely during this period, having no fellowship. One night in her dreams an old man came to her. Her description of him sounded just like 'the ancient days' in Daniel 7:9. He said to her, 'Do not worry, my child, ask me your questions and I will answer them.' For a long period after that the old man would come to her in her dreams and answer her questions.

Hilda was overjoyed to have Pavitri's help and companionship. Pavitri did much to save Hilda from making many mistakes in a new place, for Pavitri knew her own people. And Pavitri's position as a Christian was strengthened by having Hilda there. Together they began to see the medical work expand and interest in the Gospel grow.

Then the blow came. Hilda received a summons to go to Kathmandu: her visa had been cancelled. She went to Singha Durbar, the government building, and was told that reports had come in about her activities in West No. 4 district, and while these were being investigated she must stay in Kathmandu.

While she waited, she helped at the United Mission hospital in Kathmandu. She went almost daily to the government offices for news. She didn't quite know how to take it when at last she went into the office and was told what the government had found out about her. In reply to their enquiries about her Christian activities in the village, the village council had reported that she had never undertaken any such activities!

Some days later the Nepali Health Minister summoned her to his office. He was very angry with her—almost frothing at the mouth, Hilda said later. He banged his hand on the table and said to her, 'I can assure you, Miss Steele, you will never return to West No. 4.'

A very crestfallen Hilda returned to her friends at the United Mission that night. However, God was at work. When the villagers heard that Hilda was not to come back to them, they wrote protesting, 'Give us back our grandmother or find us someone else!'

Shortly afterwards, the Health Minister who had spoken so angrily to Hilda developed a severe gastric ulcer and was never able to return to his post. Her application papers were considered again by a new Health Minister, and he granted her a visa to return to West No. 4. She never had any further trouble in getting a visa. The time she spent in Kathmandu had given her friends in the United Mission to Nepal who were to be invaluable to her in the future.

Shortly after Hilda's return to Pyersingh, the local council offered her and Pavitri a choice of several different sites on which to build a dispensary. After looking at them all, they decided on a beautiful site set high on a hill above Pyersingh, with a view one way looking out on the Annapurna range, and the other looking across the valley to villages nestled in the far hillside. On a clear day you could see the hill behind the Tansen hospital, forty-eight miles away. The site was at the top of a jungle path above the school. It was on four levels of terraces. The local people promised free labour to help them build the dispensary. In January 1961, I went out with two Nepali Christians from Tansen to attend the dedication of the land.

I had had previous links with Hilda in England and Ireland. I was becoming more and more involved in her work in Pyersingh. When she first started the dispensary she was not qualified, so she could not buy any drugs without a doctor's signature. She asked Carl Friedericks in Tansen if he would countersign her drug order. Instead of doing this, Carl suggested that she get her drugs from me, as I was running the medical store at the time.

However, drugs do not jump from Tansen to Pyersingh unaided. It was necessary for someone to deal with the orders, so I virtually became her agent in Tansen. Beside medicine, she also needed food, money, stationery and a forwarding address for letters as there were no shops or postal services in Pyersingh.

Hilda sent in Nepali runners every two or three weeks. It took them two days to walk the forty-eight miles in, and then two or three days back with the loads. When the men arrived—and we never quite knew when they were coming—we had to rush round and get the medicine and supplies ready and send them back to Hilda and Pavitri as soon as possible. The men never wanted to stay long because of the difficulty of being away from their farms. Someone said it was like putting a match to an anthill when Hilda's men arrived, the way we all rushed round to get everything loaded up to send out on the men's backs!

The number of believers in Pyersingh was growing, and with the new dispensary built, patients were increasing to seventy or eighty a day. There was also the farm work. Pavitri kept goats, chickens and a buffalo, and she planted crops of millet and maize on additional land they had now bought.

Hilda was feeling increasingly unable to cope on her own with the dispensary. In Tansen new people were coming, some with social-work training. Was I meant to move on and help her?

10

I Go To Pyersingh

I was an Interserve missionary working under the United Mission to Nepal. Hilda was answerable only to the local Nepali village council. She and the work were supported by gifts from friends at home. As Pyersingh was not in an area where the UMN had permission to work, it was not possible for them to take over the Pyersingh project, though it was discussed. In the end, I was seconded from the UMN hospital in Tansen to work in Pyersingh. It was one of many examples of how missionaries in Nepal have supported others' work, even work outside their own organisation.

At that time Tansen was a day's walk from the nearest bus route, and Pyersingh was a further two or three days' trek into the mountains beyond that. The trail led through beautiful scenery with superb views of the Annapurna range. At one place there was a lovely rhododendron forest, with trees rising over fifty feet. I knew the first part of the trail well, as I had often taken it to visit the mud-thatched villages where some of our TB and leprosy patients lived. The trail also went past the government leprosarium which we visited regularly from Tansen. One hill we had to climb to get there was called the 'big up'. For any hill to be called that in Nepal you know you are in for a steep climb! An enterprising Nepali erected a shack and served tea half way up.

I remember one hot May day when an Australian doctor and I broke all records returning from the leprosarium by taking the longest time ever! We only kept ourselves going by pointing out the next tree we'd make it to so we could sit in its shade. On the 'big up' it was the thought of the tea shop that kept us going. Imagine our dismay when we arrived to find the proprietor gone! We could have sat down and wept. Our reactions were so often out of proportion to the situation. Nepalis watching us could see it too.

We tried to do the forty-eight miles between Tansen and Pyersingh in two days. This meant early starts and late stops. We usually spent the first night in a Thakali hut above the Kali Gandaki river. The Thakali people are the innkeepers of Nepal, and build these huts of mud and bamboo to house passing travellers. They provide an excellent meal of rice and curry and a straw mat to sleep on.

From there it was a steep, winding descent down to the river, very slippery in the monsoon season (June to October). The river had to be crossed in a hollowed-out tree-trunk canoe. You had to stand up in it! The men who owned the canoes lived nearby and would paddle us across. After that we had to wade fourteen times across the river back and forth. One time in the monsoon season, Hilda and I were crossing the river during pouring rain. The river was a torrent, the water high above our waists, and we were having trouble crossing. Hilda was carrying a bottle of boiled drinking water (it was never safe to drink unboiled water).

In the middle of the river we met a group of Nepalis crossing in the opposite direction. Seeing the bottle they asked what was in it, hoping no doubt that it would be the local potent liquor, 'raksi', which is the same colour as water. When Hilda said 'water', they stopped and stared at us in amazement. 'Water?' they said. 'What do you want with water?' We could see their point. Here we were, up to our necks in water, with more pouring from the skies, and yet we were carrying it in a bottle. These foreigners were hard to figure out!

After wading across the river there was a four-hour walk uphill, the last part of which led through a forest. The first time I went, the men got lost. We walked to and fro in the forest for two hours, trying to find the path. The only light we had was my torch. When I could stand it no longer I asked the men what they thought we should do if we didn't find the path soon? They cheerfully said, 'Oh, we can walk about all night and at dawn we'll be able to see where we are.' It was the end of a long, two-day trek, and I was in no mood to walk about all night!

I sat down by the side of the road and asked God to have mercy on us, particularly on me, though I was not carrying the load. He did. We found the path and arrived late, but safe, at Pavitri and Hilda's house. They had not been worried. You never knew in Nepal if, or when, your visitors would arrive.

Two of our friends from Tansen not only got lost but lost their carriers too. They had somehow got separated from them and then wandered off the main path—not difficult to do. They had no idea where to go; they felt as if they were in the middle of nowhere. There were no houses, and no one to ask. They were about to despair when, from behind a bush, a child of about ten bobbed up and said, 'Jaya Masih,' the Christian greeting! They were astounded, because apart from us they didn't know that there were any Christians in the area. This child and her family belonged to our church, but lived in a village about three hours' walk from Pyersingh. They were the only ones in the area then.

The child, who had been out cutting grass, took them to her home where they were given some much-needed refreshment. The mother then let the child go with them as a guide to Pyersingh. There was no way they would have got there on their own. Hilda, who was just about to send out a search party, was very relieved to see them. The carriers had already arrived, and were agitated that their 'charges' had not turned up.

Pyersingh was an important village which had its own headman. There was one shop. The proprietor had rice, cigarettes, sugar, spices, soap, small combs and other goods, carried in from Pokhara.

There was a school, to which children from surrounding villages came. There was also a flat area in front of the school which had been made into a basketball pitch. A short, flat street of mud, with houses on one side and a steep ravine on the other, comprised the centre of the village. Otherwise the people lived in houses perched on the side of the hills. Everyone had small or larger pieces of land, on which they farmed. They grew millet and maize, and kept goats, buffaloes and chickens. At that time the area was heavily forested, and deer could be seen. As there was virtually no flat land, the farmers terraced it.

When Hilda moved onto the new land they had been given, the villagers built a small house for her.

She wrote of this: 'My new house—it couldn't really be called a house—even Pavitri said, "It isn't a human dwelling, it isn't a stable; what is it?"—is far too small. So I have no privacy, nor has Pavitri, and the dispensary space is inadequate. We shall certainly have to enlarge at the first opportunity, when the monsoon is over!'

A few months later, they were able to do this, and again Hilda wrote: 'We have started on the building of a large hut—this will have a thatch roof and be in the same style as that in which I lived in Pokhara. I confess, I long for the day when I can be possessive, and say, "my room" and close a door. The supervision of the work falls on me. I have to watch each post, or it is out of line or crooked. Also, I want space now, and local opinion runs to "making do" with a very small area. I still have to be very stubborn about windows, and having the doorways high enough for a six-foot person to avoid bumping his head. The generosity of one of [the Lord's] saints, and the most helpful co-operation of [Christians] in Tansen have provided me with two beds, two chairs and a table, and there will be cupboards and bookcases later. I have had my old desk sent out from Pokhara, so very shortly I'll have quite a comfy little home.'

The local folks later built Hilda a dispensary, and also a room over it where Pavitri's sister, Saili, slept. Pavitri had another room over a goat shed. There was a hen house below the dispensary, and a buffalo shed to one side. Hilda's house was on a higher terrace above the dispensary. The house was a long, mud-and-stone building with a thatched roof. The doors and windows were wooden frames covered with plastic sheeting. The windows could be pushed out and kept open with sticks. The hut (for that, virtually, was what it was) was divided into two halves by a curtain, one half being Hilda's bedroom, the other the sitting room.

A small portion was partitioned off for a bathroom, consisting of a plastic bowl on a bamboo stand. Sam, a Peace Corps man from America, came to stay with Hilda to get over the shock of his friend being killed on one of the Nepali paths. While he was with her, he got the local people to help him to make an arrangement to pipe water onto the land from a nearby spring. Considering he was an academic (he later became a lawyer in New York) Sam did an excellent job, but the plastic pipe often became blocked, so thirsty Nepali goatherds would cut it to have a drink. We were always having to go out to fix it. An American engineer who saw our contorted pipe said, 'The only thing one can say is, it works, but how it does I don't understand.' It did work, and it served us well over the years.

Outside at the back was a small stone building which was the toilet. This consisted of a deep hole topped by a wooden box with a loo seat on it. We had to change the box at frequent intervals because the white ants tended to eat it, or it would just begin to rot during the rainy season. The hole used to fill up quite quickly, especially when we had visitors. One of the features of the toilet that our visitors remarked on were the large, long-legged spiders that hung around and watched people sit in there. We regarded them as friends, but our visitors were not so sure.

It became one of my jobs to empty the hole before and after visitors came, and to bury the contents in the garden. It filled up so quickly, and there wasn't any suitable ground around to build a fresh one. One of the arguments the Nepalis used for not making toilets was that the manure would be lost to their fields. However, I mostly gave up the battle to get toilets built, though I did tell people that they should at least follow the example of cats, who knew enough to cover their droppings.

Next to Hilda's hut was the kitchen, and beyond that, joined to it by a mud-and-stone partition, was my bedroom. I used to keep an oil primus stove there, so that if Pavitri was delayed with the animals, as she frequently was, I could cook a meal on it. The only other cooking facility we had, which Pavitri used in the kitchen, was a hollowed-out depression in the mud floor with a metal tripod placed over it into which we fed firewood. We had no heating. In the cold weather we used to take up the mats in the sitting room and light a log fire on the mud floor.

Many people came to the dispensary and to the house. Pavitri belonged to the dominant Magar tribe of the village, and a lot of those who came to visit us were Magars. At the time, Magars didn't eat buffalo meat, so we didn't cook it in our kitchen. Neither did we allow outcastes into the kitchen. If we had let them in, no one else could have eaten at our house. The headman thanked us for having respect for their customs as it would have made it very difficult for the villagers if we had not.

We were, however, criticised for not demonstrating the liberty we have in Christ. But Paul says in 1 Corinthians 8:8-9 and 13 that we should not let our liberty be a stumbling-block to others. The path between liberty and restraint is a narrow one. As for our 'liberty' to eat meat, it wasn't available anyway—

unless we killed our own animals, and somehow we weren't keen to eat animals we had known by name.

I had a special chicken once, which seemed more like an ostrich than a chicken and looked as if it wore glasses. I called it 'Specs'. It followed me everywhere. About that time I contracted hepatitis and became severely ill. Hilda was hard put to know what to feed me. One evening she gave me chicken, a good choice to build up my strength. Some days later, when I was feeling better, I enquired which chicken she had killed. Rather shamefacedly she said, 'Specs.' It was the only chicken we had that was ready for the pot. It was no use being sentimental. However, I was glad that I was too sick on the night I ate 'Specs' to realise what I was doing. Hilda was glad too!

Every year we held a local fair in the village, which Hilda had actually initiated. One year a local man came to me and said, 'I will get you some meat.' He took me to the house of a lady I knew well. She looked at the man and then at me, and said, 'I am sorry I can't give it to you, it has been offered to idols.' I wished she hadn't told me; if you don't know the meat has been offered to an idol, it's OK to eat it! I would have loved some meat about then.

We were always reminded that we lived in the midst of a Hindu community. Hilda had once been a chicken farmer. To improve the egg yield and increase the size of the chickens around Pyersingh, she bought some Rhode Island Red cocks. This was no mean achievement, as they had to be carried for three days on men's backs, fed and watered at regular intervals— and all that after surviving the long train and bus journey from Gorakhpur in India, where they had been purchased.

As a gesture of friendship and encouragement, she gave a cock to the headman in each part of the village. She hoped that they would use the cocks to breed a better strain of bird, and that they would be inspired to improve the stock throughout the village. Sadly Hilda underestimated the Nepali's love of feasting. What was worse, Hilda distributed the cocks a few months before the biggest Hindu festival of the year!

The cocks grew large and had plenty of flesh on them. It was true that they might have sired larger birds, but there was no certainty they would, and anyway, they might be eaten by a jungle cat before then—so why keep them for an uncertain future when the need was here and now? Before Hilda could do anything, into the cooking pot went all her precious Rhode Island Red cocks on the big feast day. Only the ones she had kept herself survived.

One night at about 11:30 pm, the dog got restless and started to growl. When he didn't stop, Hilda got up and went to investigate. She saw figures in the hen run. She went down as quickly as she could, but by the time she arrived the intruders were fleeing. By the light of her torch she saw people racing down the mountainside carrying her cocks and hens with them. There was no way, at that time of night, that she could go after them.

Next day the village elders came up to Hilda, very ashamed of what had happened. Hilda was pretty sure she knew who had done it, and that they did not belong to the village. To Hilda's dismay, the headman said that for the honour of the village they must find out who did it. She realised that this would probably involve the use of sorcery.

Sure enough, up came the witch doctor in all his war paint and regalia. He took up his position in the chicken run, in spite of Hilda's protests. He then picked up one of the birds the thieves had not taken, mumbled some incantations over it, whirled it around his head several times and then released it. The bird immediately flew straight down the hillside, heading for the village from which Hilda was pretty certain the thieves had come. The whole village then rushed in hot pursuit of the hen. Some time later, the headman came up and offered Hilda money to compensate her for the loss of her cocks and hens. They had found the thieves, but the birds had already been eaten. Hilda refused to take the money.

We not only had problems with human invaders in the hen run, but also with wild animals, particularly jungle cats. One night there was a sudden call from Pavitri. It was pouring with rain. We all rushed down to the hen run. There was a large jungle cat inside, trying to kill the birds who were rushing hither and thither in a great frenzy. Hilda had picked up a large stick on the way down and she started to hit what she thought was the cat. It was dark and difficult to see. Suddenly Pavitri called out, 'It's the cock you are hitting, not the cat!' I gathered up the cock under my arm. I already had one of our dogs under the other; he'd been no help at all, simply rushing around and adding to the confusion.

We all knew that if we didn't kill the cat it would get all our chickens. Eventually the other dog, who unlike the one under my arm had amazing courage and sense, managed to pin the cat in a corner, and between them—Hilda, Pavitri and the dog—they killed it.

Hilda, as an agriculturalist, longed to improve the lot of the farmers in the area. So she obtained a large Israeli goat. He was to improve the size of the local goats so that people, among other things, could sell them for more money.

This goat was a great white beast with enormous horns. 'Horn' in Nepali is 'singh', so Amma (Pavitri's mother) called him 'Singapore'. This was a place known to all Nepalis, because some Gurkha regiments were stationed there. Singapore lived to a ripe old age. We never ate him! He sired many white and mottled goats. Local people brought their goats and paid half a rupee for his services. His offspring, however, were not too popular because they tended to be too big for the young goatherds to handle.

Another innovation Hilda tried was growing three crops a year. Most farmers grew two, millet and corn. We also tried growing wheat. To make it a viable proposition for the local people we didn't hire labour but did it ourselves. It was a rush to get one crop harvested, the ground manured and prepared for the next crop, and that sown. At some times in the year we could hardly move about in the house for corn and millet! It was hard work, and it was by no means the only thing we did. Sadly, after Hilda left, very few farmers grew wheat as an extra crop. Many of them, however, did grow lentils around the edge of their fields. Hilda had encouraged this, as lentils provided needed protein for their diet.

Hilda enjoyed the agricultural side of the work and was happiest when in the fields or garden. She could have been the author of that saying: 'You are nearer to God in a garden than anywhere else on earth.'

For Pavitri, too, the more goats we had the happier she was. She once said to me, 'I like things in large numbers.' She also loved buffaloes, though happily we never had more than two of those. They are not my favourite animal. However, it was through two buffaloes that I experienced the power we have in the name of Jesus over the forces of Satan.

One day I was on my own with Pavitri and her old mother. We were in the midst of a Hindu festival. Someone had sent me a card on which was written: 'Your God reigns.' I was meditating on these words early in the morning, and asking God how he could reign with all the turmoil and worship of heathen gods going on below us in the village.

I suddenly heard Pavitri's mother, Amma, crying, 'Nani, nani'—which means, 'Child, child.' I realised she was calling Pavitri, but getting no response.

I rushed out of my bedroom and called out, 'Amma, what is it?'

She said, 'The buffalo, the buffalo!' As it was obvious that Pavitri was not about, I ran down to the buffalo shed. I found our two big buffaloes on the ground with their heads together, their horns over each other's throats; they were throttling each other. How they got like that we shall never know. Their tongues were hanging out and their eyes protruding! As we lived in the forest well above the village, there was no one I could call. I asked Amma if she had her cutting knife with her. However, she was leading Singapore, the big goat, to a place of safety. (He shared the buffalo shed then.)

So I rushed for our bread knife to cut the halters, which I thought were also choking them. It was a stupid thing to do, as it freed them from being fixed to their posts in the ground. They rose up together, their horns still linked over each other's throats. They became desperate and started to rear up and down, trying to get free of each other. They were big animals and, to my horror, began to knock the shed down in their frenzy!

I was standing, staring helplessly at them, when I heard a voice. 'Huh, so your God reigns does he? I reign here and these buffaloes are going to die, and what sort of witness will that be to the power of your God?' (The Hindus believe that gods afflict you, but if you placate them enough they will also protect you and yours.)

I mustered what strength I could and cried out, 'Satan, get out in the name of Jesus Christ. You have no part here; this place belongs to Jesus, and he reigns here, not you!'

I watched with amazement as the two big buffaloes fell at my feet and remained there like lambs. Their horns were still locked over each other's throats, their eyes bulging and their tongues hanging out. I knelt down beside them and got hold of their horns, trying to force them apart to free them. I was praying as hard as I could, with my understanding and in tongues. It seemed as if they would never be free. Just as my strength was giving out, Pavitri arrived back. She had been out cutting grass for them. I called to her and she came immediately to help. With our combined strength we managed to get the horns over their heads.

Once freed, they stood up as if nothing had happened. They were unharmed apart from one of them having got a scratch on his face. I, on the other hand, was completely shaken and needed some brandy! (We had a bottle for emergencies.)

Pavitri could not understand what had happened. When she had gone out, about half an hour before, the buffaloes had been meekly standing together in their stalls. Neither she nor the pastor had any difficulty believing it was a satanic attack against us. The pastor even said, 'Oh well, Satan has horns, hasn't he?' I wondered where he learnt that. For my part, I was grateful to have been able to prove the power of Jesus' name in a new way.

The agricultural work was probably what I liked least about my move to Pyersingh. I had been born and bred in London, and apart from cats, rabbits, guinea pigs and a tortoise, I had never been around animals.

In the evening we used to let the chickens out. During that time we often banged a tin tray to scare off the jungle cats and foxes. It was one of the jobs you might be given to do if you visited us. On occasions we had larger animals, such as leopards, prowling around too. One day we saw a mother leopard and her cub coming up the path to our land, but hearing our tin-tray banging efforts, she turned round and disappeared the other way.

During one period we had too much goat manure, so we would send it down for Pavitri's land in Paimey, two hours away. A man who was rather dim used to carry it down for us in sacks on his back. As the manure had been dug out from under the goats, stalks and sticks from their food were usually mixed in it. If we had left them in, it would have meant a very uncomfortable load for the man. So one of our morning jobs was to take the stalks and sticks out of the manure and then put the manure into sacks ready for the man when he came. He had two hours' walk each way.

I can remember feeling very frustrated and saying to God, 'I didn't come to Nepal to take sticks out of manure. It can't be furthering the work of your kingdom for us to be sitting here doing this! It's not as if we can talk to the man about you; he doesn't seem to understand anything.'

I was wrong. There is no limit to the means God can use. That man's wife, his three sons, two daughters and their husbands are all Christians now. One daughter is helping in the dispensary, and one son has passed his School Leaving Certificate and is going to train as a vet. And our initial contact with the family was through the father carrying manure!

One of the 'things' over the years that used to get me worked up were the missionaries who wanted more time to do 'spiritual work'. I knew that those who were most respected and valued by the Nepalis were those who worked hard and conscientiously, and were always there in a crisis ready to get their hands dirty. They were usually given the Bible studies and prayer meetings to run as well. As my manure story shows, God can use anything for the furtherance of his kingdom! If to further his kingdom is our heart's desire, he will give us opportunities in everything we do.

There is a large group among mission supporters at home who expect most of a missionary's work to be 'spiritual'. One supporter who visited us thought we rushed about but achieved very little. We ourselves often felt that way. So we were naturally encouraged whenever we saw any spiritual response or sign of spiritual life. Other supporters, however, expect 'spiritual life' to be shown in good works. This is scriptural. The fact is, all Christian work is spiritual. God uses us whether we are picking sticks out of manure or leading Bible classes. God is honoured when we trust and obey him; that is all that counts.

In Nepal there was never this division between 'spiritual work' and other work. Supporting agencies in the western world have arisen in differing contexts and make their appeals to different sections of the community. Some are denominational, some appeal to a wider public by emphasising the humanitarian aspects of their work, while others find it important to stress their evangelistic basis. But when John the Baptist challenged Jesus about his ministry he was not given a 'theological' reply, but told to look at the practical (and miraculous!) ways in which the good news was being announced to the poor. So in Nepal those western distinctions and sensitivities were largely irrelevant. We often didn't know what sending agency was supporting the others, or what denomination they belonged to. It was enough that for the love of Jesus we tried to face every need that confronted us.

Coming home, it has been disappointing to find people defending their own patch or denomination so strongly, labelling those they disagree with, and setting up rivalries and competitiveness such as we read about in 1 Corinthians 1,10-13. Sadly, this has become more evident in Nepal as the church has grown, and is a poor reflection of a kingdom where the Master was a servant and his servants are called to esteem others as better than themselves.

11

Further Pyersingh Insights

After Hilda had moved out of the old school house into her new house above the dispensary, the villagers decided to reopen the school and begin classes. Everyone in the village was approached to help with the funds. Donations were to be given according to income. The parents of the children going to school were charged a small sum each month. The really poor were allowed free schooling at the discretion of the village council. The school flourished, and drew in about 200 children.

By government order—and to the sadness of the village—a beautiful large tree in the centre of the village had to be cut down and the ground cleared to make a volley-ball pitch in front of the school.

At first the masters were mostly local men, and over the years they were the ones that kept the school going, as others, appointed from outside, came and went. The villagers sent mainly their boys to school, as education was not thought necessary for girls who, after all, only got married! Usually less than five per cent of the students were girls. Since Nepal was becoming more bureaucratic and forms were frequently appearing which needed filling in, most families thought it necessary for their sons, at least, to be able to read and write. However, once they had learned to do this, they were usually taken out of school and put to work in the fields.

I was sad not to be allowed to teach more English at the school. I did for a time, but was stopped; the school committee said I was having a Christian influence. I never referred to Christianity in class. I only taught very elementary English, such as: 'How are you?' 'I am fine'; 'How are you?' 'I am fine, too' – which merely followed the syllabus book!

The children knew us because we held a free school clinic on Wednesday afternoons, where we treated any accidents that took place during school hours. Parents coming to the clinic with their children often admitted that they had wanted to take them to the witch doctor, but the children had insisted on coming to us. The children who came to the clinic were often quite mischievous, getting medicines not just for themselves but also for their families. Sometimes we even learned that they were selling their medicine to other people. Therefore we got into the habit of giving them their worm medicine on the spot, and made them come for their ear drops daily.

If any of the children wandered where they weren't supposed to on our land, our little Tibetan dog would go after them. One of his favourite pastimes was to chase them all up the trees and keep them there until we came to rescue them. There grew to be quite a love-hate relationship between them.

I also taught older people to read and write; this was later developed as non-formal education. I enjoyed this, for most of them were eager to learn, especially if they had become Christians and wanted to read the Bible.

Beside the non-formal education, school clinics

and agricultural work, we had busy dispensaries. People walked many hours to come; there were often eighty or 100 patients a day. We had all sorts of cases, from typhoid and malaria to worms, diarrhoea, eye and ear diseases and skin conditions. We also had TB and leprosy patients, gynaecological and obstetric cases—and, of course, the accidents, which could vary from falls from slippery paths to hands getting caught in rice-pounding machines.

Our maternity cases were never normal deliveries; women came only when there were problems. Pavitri worked a lot with Hilda on these cases. She went to Tansen for several months' training with a Norwegian sister there. As she had never been to school, she couldn't get formal training. Over the years, however, she became expert at abnormal delivery cases. I would rather have worked with her on these cases than with some highly trained doctor or midwife straight from a western country. I remember once coming back from Paimey with a Canadian doctor. Pavitri described to him a case she had just delivered on the floor of the local shop, and added, 'I wish you'd been there.' The doctor said, 'Phew, I couldn't have done it. I'm glad I wasn't there!'

Life was never dull. We had no idea what would happen next. One day an eight-foot snake came into the house. Fortunately, its head caught in some netting, so it was easier for us to kill. Another time the dog led us to a venomous snake which we'd had around for three weeks and were at last able to kill. Once a poisonous snake hid under the prayer mats and slid over Hilda's hand when she picked them up.

If we went out, we never knew what kind of case might be waiting for us when we got back. The fight against disease and against the powers of darkness and ignorance never left us. Hilda, in one of her letters, had this to say:

We have had a very strenuous time on the medical side of the work—big clinics and many calls out to cases. We reckon some thirty miles were covered last week, and it looks as if it will be just as heavy this week. Oh, the tragedy we often see! One day a very precious only son of five was carried in, dying. He had been ill, and the parents had bought and given 'medicine' which produced chaotic symptoms. We feared he would die in the dispensary. We sent him home alive, and the parents were carefully instructed how to give our treatment. It was a big disappointment to us when, forty-eight hours later, the father came and told us that his neighbours had said we did not understand this 'illness', and he had stopped treatment. However, he did come to tell us. Using Pavitri as our spokeswoman, we tried to teach him the foolishness of superstition and of listening to everyone's advice! He brought the child again, and under the good hand of God he has made a little progress and we hope and pray he will live now.

A case that deeply saddened us was that of a young woman in a village several hours' walk from here. She gave birth to premature twins and had a retained placenta. We were not called for five days. The path to their home is very steep and difficult. We found the patient with high fever and other complications. It had been promised that a man would see us safely home and carry our kit for us. He left us half way. We were very weary when we got home in the dark. No one came for further medicines for her, and later we heard that she died three days after our visit.

Putuli, Pavitri's sister-in-law, had her first baby prematurely, and it only lived a few minutes. Churya, a brother-in-law, got ill with a liver abscess. With these last events, the villagers in Paimey are jeering, and saying, Where is your God? The woman died, Putuli's baby died, and Churya is ill. All very real tests of faith for us all.

I will never forget the day when Hilda and I were called out to two cases in two different directions from the dispensary. We set off to go to the first one, about an hour's walk away. We had to go down the side of the mountain and along a very barren track. As we got down onto the main path we caught up with a party leading a buffalo they had just bought. They asked us not to pass them, as the buffalo was very temperamental. The drop off the trail was precipitous at that point, and knowing something of the unpredictability of buffaloes, we remained walking behind them. Then we saw another group hurrying toward us carrying what was obviously a patient. The buffalo party called out to the oncomers to stop until they had passed them. They explained there was no point in hurrying anyway, as there was no one at the dispensary, since we were on the path behind them.

In spite of this warning, the oncoming party took no notice, and with the patient in a hammock fixed to a pole carried by two men, they kept coming on, in no way heeding the cries from the buffalo party to stop. We could see little from where we were as to what happened, but before we knew it there was a mighty scream, and to our horror we saw the buffalo plunging down the side of the cliff to its certain death.

As you can imagine, pandenomium broke out between the two groups. As we ourselves were on an urgent call, and since we could contribute nothing to the argument, we went on. We saw our patient, and then went to the second patient to whom we had been called on the other side of the village. To our dismay, while tending the second patient, we heard the Hindu death wail from the dispensary hill. That could have only one meaning; the lady we had met earlier on the trail had just died.

We retraced our steps to the dispensary as quickly as we could. The buffalo party had gone (we never heard if they got any settlement or not). The woman was dead. The people with her didn't appear to be upset about her death so much as about the fact that she had died on Christian ground, and that our hens had tried to run over her! It has always interested me what different priorities people have in life.

The day was even more memorable for Hilda and myself, because not only did the woman and the buffalo die, but also the two patients whom we had visited.

Five years later, when Hilda was not there, that day was to have repercussions for me. I arrived back earlier than I had expected after walking the twenty-six miles over very mountainous country from Pokhara. I was hot and tired. As I came in view of the dispensary, I saw a crowd of Nepalis on the lowest terrace of our land. I went around the corner and met Pavitri and Saili, her sister, standing staring down at the people below.

'Who are they and what are they doing here?' I asked.

'You remember the woman who died on the verandah five years ago?' (How could I forget?) 'Well, they say her spirit is still here, and they have come with the Hindu priest to drive it away. They wanted to do it on the verandah where she had died, but I wouldn't let them. I made them go as low down on our land as they could.'

As I have said, I was hot and tired, and suddenly I was very angry too. How dare they take advantage of Pavitri while she was on her own! They knew I would not have given permission, so they must have planned this. As they were the top religious and secular leaders in the area, they knew it would be extremely difficult for Pavitri, a Nepali village woman, to refuse them. So, without thinking, I stormed down to tell them exactly what I thought of them.

When I got down to where they were I found they had taken down one of our fences. I raised my voice and asked them what they thought they were doing on our land. They began to explain, apologise and make excuses. Higher up in the house my little pug-nosed Tibetan dog, Yeti, realised I was back and rushed down to greet me. He had heard my raised voice, so he thought I might need his help. Before I could do anything, he had rushed at all those high-up men, going from one to the other, barking and biting their legs! I tried, to no avail, to call him off. Then to my amazement, all the men proceeded to climb up the trees!

I gathered up Yeti, who was still barking furiously, and putting him under my arm, stood and surveyed the scene. All the high-ups of the area, in their best clothes, were perched up in the trees around me. They begged me to take the dog away. I replied I would only do so if they replaced my fence and did their Hindu worship elsewhere. It wouldn't work on our Christian land anyway.

Without hesitation they agreed to fix the fence and

leave. Yeti was still protesting loudly from under my arm as I turned and walked slowly up the hill.

From the upper terrace I watched while they removed all their paraphernalia, put the fence back up, and went into an adjacent piece of land to do their ceremony. When I cooled down and had time to reflect on what I had done, I realised I had probably angered all the headmen of the area. They had all been there. I might easily lose my visa. An adverse report from them would mean that I wouldn't get it next year.

I was not surprised when later in the afternoon I saw our headman walking up the path. I went down to greet him. After the usual pleasantries I asked him to come up and have a cup of tea. Over the tea and biscuits I waited for what might come. However, he made no reference to the morning's activities. Instead, he said, 'In previous years we have always given you a tree from the forest for firewood. We haven't done so yet this year, but if one of you would like to come with me some time, I will show you which tree you can have.' I thanked him politely and said I would arrange to go with him to see the tree some time. After a few more pleasantries on both sides, he departed. Over the next few days other participants of the morning fracas came to see me at the dispensary. I had never seen them so deferential.

The local village council was usually very helpful to us. The dog prior to Yeti, named Rintin, got very ill, and Hilda was sure he had rabies. His legs became paralysed and he developed symptoms of hydrophobia. At that time there was no rabies vaccine in Pokhara, so for treatment we had to go to Gorakhpur across the border in India, a trip of four or five days. We all ran a great risk of contracting the disease.

However, Hilda decided she was not going to go for vaccination. Pavitri and Saili also were adamant that they weren't going. But Hilda said I had to go, because she was answerable to Interserve and UMN for me! I protested and said, 'What do you think I'll feel like if I go and come back in about three weeks (the treatment was ten days of injections into your stomach) and find you all dead with rabies?' However, they all insisted that they would stay and that I should go. Then followed one of the worst twenty-four hours of my life.

How I prayed! Rintin got worse. Then the headman came up to see us, and Hilda asked him if he thought Rintin had rabies. He looked at the dog, heard his history, and said, 'I've seen many cases of rabies and I'm sure this dog hasn't got it.'

What a relief! Even after this some doubt remained, as Rintin died within ten days of the onset of his illness. (If a dog lives longer than ten days, you can be sure it didn't have rabies.) So he could have died of it. It was also little comfort at the time to read an article saying that rabies could develop up to three years after handling a rabid dog!

He was a lovely little dog. We buried him in the garden. We never did know what he died of.

12

Daniel and the Lions' Den

It was a joy for us when people became Christians. We were awed at the cost they were prepared to pay to do so.

When Pavitri first became a Christian none of her family showed any interest. In fact, they were antagonistic. Her own mother was among those who excommunicated her from the village. As time went on, however, they began to realise that Jesus came to this world for the Nepali people as well as for westerners.

In 1963 Pavitri's mother, Amma, and her two friends, Lillawatti and Shanta Kumari, arrived to spend Christmas with us. They arrived bringing gifts: vegetables they had grown, eggs, and a cloth one of them had embroidered. They were skilled at embroidery, using local patterns that had been handed down from generation to generation. They also brought a live chicken (we never had a dead one brought to us). The three women were all poor, but they never came empty-handed. They were all over seventy, bent and wrinkled, but still able to walk the two hours over the mountains to reach us. They were delighted to be with us, and we were delighted to have them.

Amma was the leader; it was she who had finally convinced them to follow Christ, not an easy thing for any of them.

In the evening, after a meal of rice and curry together, we all sat on straw mats on the mud floor around a smoky wood fire in the kitchen, which was the only sitting place we had at the time. Although the space was cramped, we could have sat all night listening to those three old ladies telling how they had done everything they knew in Hinduism—made sacrifices, paid homage to idols, given money to the priests, gone on pilgrimages to sacred shrines—and yet never could find peace. But now that they had met with Jesus, they knew that no further pilgrimages were necessary to find the truth and the living God.

Each one had stories of how Jesus had revealed himself to them, and they spoke of his help and nearness.

Lillawatti was a childless widow, a real tough old lady. She died before she could be baptised. Her Hindu relatives made life very difficult for her, but she was staunch in her faith to the end. She said one day to Hilda, 'If I die first I will wait for you at the gate of heaven; if you die first, please be on the lookout for me.'

These days I often picture Lillawatti as I knew her, in her best Magar red velvet blouse with the tie crossed over the front and a dark piece of cloth wrapped round her lower half, the two held together by a long piece of material wound many times round her middle. I can see her bent body, and her beady eyes peering out of heaven looking for Hilda's coming. Ridiculous I know, but one does picture the dead as one knew them. I can now picture her delight as, since starting to write this, Hilda has died.

Amma had always been a highly respected member of the community, so when she became a Christian she had greater problems. Every year at the annual Dasai Hindu festival the villagers came to her to have her place the red tika mark on their foreheads. This was a sign that you were accepting the blessing of the Hindu gods. Amma didn't know what to do, so she decided to ask Hilda and Pavitri for advice.

She got ready to walk up and see them, but as she came out of the house she felt as if God put a restraining hand on her shoulder and said, 'Why do you have to go and ask your daughter? You can ask me; I am here with you.' So she turned around and went up by herself to sit in the jungle to hear what God would say to her. Later Amma said to me, 'Do you know God speaks Magar?'

Magar is the tribal language that Amma speaks. In the church, however, the national language, Nepali, is used, so up to then Amma had never heard anyone pray aloud in Magar. She had presumed, therefore, that God didn't understand her tribal language. She said with awe, 'I heard him speak to me in my own language. Have you ever felt the softness of his wings around you? I felt I was nestling under his wings. He told me what I should do when the people came for the tika. I can't explain how he told me but I knew what I was to do.'

The next day when her neighbours came, she said to them, 'I can no longer put a tika on your foreheads, because I no longer believe in the Hindu gods. I now trust in the living God.' Then she said to me, 'I told them about Jesus, and how he loved them and gave his life for them, and how I could bless them in the name of Jesus.' This she did, putting a cross on their foreheads 'in the name of the Father, Son and Holy

Spirit'. All the neighbours were pleased to accept the blessing she gave them.

Talking about it afterwards, Hilda and I were interested that God told her to put something on their foreheads; we would probably have felt it was too like the old tika to advise her to do that. We wouldn't have been as brave as God was! We might well have advised against a confrontation. Not for the first time were we thankful that God knew better than we did how to teach people about himself.

It was an unspeakable privilege for us to be present at Amma's baptism. Pastor David decided she was too old to take down to the river to be immersed, so the baptism took place in Pavitri's room. Goats, chickens, cats and a dog were all present too. Pastor David took our thoughts back to the first upper room, and we were all conscious of the risen presence of the Lord in our midst. Amma was serene, even regal, throughout the ceremony. She certainly was a rare soul.

One surprise of the occasion was hearing Amma called by her real name, Champa Maya, since everyone always called her 'Amma', which means mother. I thought she herself looked surprised to hear herself so addressed. Pastor David kept repeating it as he asked her questions.

'Champa Maya, do you renounce sin? Champa Maya, are you willing to have nothing more to do with idols? Champa Maya, are you prepared to renounce Hinduism and follow Christ?' So the questions went on. No light matter this, being baptised. It was a real break with the past, a coming into new life in Christ.

Practices and beliefs that have been present for years are hard to give up. Christians believe in a God who is omnipresent and all-knowing. This is not so with the Hindu gods who, it is thought, can be tricked into not knowing something has happened.

Not long after Amma's baptism, her daughter-in-law had her first live baby—after a premature birth, a still birth, and a miscarriage. Amma acted as midwife, and as soon as the baby was born, she grabbed it and took it to her own daughter who already had five children. She gave the baby to her. A little while later her son, the father of the baby, went and bought his child back from his sister for one rupee.

Amma had done this to trick the Hindu gods into thinking the baby had been born to her daughter instead of her daughter-in-law. She thought the gods had put a curse on her daughter-in-law to keep her childless. If the gods found out that she had had a child, they might harm it. But Amma had forgotten that the Christian God was not like that. When she was asked about what she had done, she said, 'Well, I wasn't sure, and I thought I'd better do it just to be on the safe side.' She seemed quite relieved to realise that this sort of subterfuge was not necessary with the God in whom she had now put her trust.

On three occasions Amma was summoned by the village council to put her mark (she couldn't write) on a paper to say that she would stop being a Christian and would publicly denounce Christ. Each time they came she refused to go, informing her tormentors that they could kill her if they liked but she would not give up the religion in which she had found peace. The third time they came she said, 'You will have to come with a paper with the King's seal on it before I will go with you. If you try to force me you'll have to put a halter on me and lead me like a goat for all to see. You will have to feed me, and when I get to the office I will only put my mark to the words, "I will not cease to be a Christian." ' She told me, 'In the end they gave up when they realised I was a hopeless case.'

Since Amma refused to sign a statement giving up her new religion, her neighbours sought to undermine her faith by killing off her goats. Villagers invest their money in their livestock and in their jewellery, so this was a great loss for Amma. Amma told us, 'They came to me and said, "Old woman, why do you not weep for your goats?" ' Looking up at us with a bright smile on her face, she said, 'I told them, "Why should I weep for my goats? They would die anyway. My treasure is in the things that are eternal." '

Amma had another old friend, Rosumma, who became a Christian. One year when there was a great food shortage (not an uncommon occurrence), Rosumma got down to one large bunch of bananas—that was all she had to eat. We called those particular type of bananas 'tummy fillers' because they are large. Rosumma took the bunch of bananas, put them on a white cloth, and spread it before the Lord. She said, 'God, you promised to look after us and supply our need. I will eat one of these bananas each day, and when they are finished I will trust you to give me something to eat.' Now if I had known of Rosumma's need, I would have wanted to rush in and do something before that. But God is in the business of making gold for his kingdom. The purest gold goes through a lot of fire.

In the meantime Amma, not knowing what was happening to her old friend, set out on Rosumma's last banana day to go down the hill with her water pot to collect her water as usual from the spring below her house. On the way she had to pass her youngest daughter's house. At that time the daughter was not a believer; in fact she was antagonistic to her mother. As Amma went past her house, to her great surprise her daughter threw a bundle of grain at her feet saying, 'Here old woman, you had better have this.' Amma went on down and collected her water. Walking back, she thought about her old friend, Rosumma, and wondered how she was getting on.

She went around to her house and found her eating her last banana. So together they spread out the grain on the white cloth and thanked their heavenly Father for supplying their need.

Pavitri said later to me, 'You would have rushed in and given her something, and what a lesson of faith you would have denied her!'

I still find this business of when to give and when not to give very difficult. It would be easy, if one had nothing to give. But most of the time we had more than the Nepalis. Their need was so vast. I still struggle with it, and try not 'to shut up the bowels of my compassion' as the King James Version says. There are no easy answers.

One Christmas the local council in Paimey, where Amma lived, put pickets on the road to stop the Christians from coming up to us for a service on Christmas Day. Only two managed to come, one making her way off the road through the jungle. Amma marched straight through the pickets, saying to them, 'Who is going to stop me from going to see my daughters?' Besides Pavitri and Saili, she always regarded Hilda and me as her children.

When you have dauntless old ladies like this in the villages of Nepal, is it any wonder that now there is more freedom and that thousands are coming into the kingdom of God?

The third old lady who came that Christmas Eve was Santa Kumari. In many ways, she had the most difficult time of the three. Becoming a Christian entailed totally breaking with her home and all it stood for, because her husband was a witch doctor. For a time he read the Bible and seemed to be convinced of the truth of it. However, the pull of his old life drew him back. Later, at the same time the local council was trying to get Amma to sign that she was not a Christian, the local council came and told Santa Kumari that she would have to choose between Christ and her husband. She said, 'I cannot deny Christ; my husband will have to live separately.' Her daughter-in-law, Gomaya, stood with her in her determination to remain a Christian. The husband did move out to a house nearby. He had to cook for himself, because if Santa Kumari or Gomaya cooked for him he would become an outcaste!

The tormentors in the village tried to force these two women and Amma and her youngest daughter, Kanchi, now a Christian, to drink cow's urine in order to make them Hindus again. The cow, of course, is a sacred animal in the Hindu religion. When they refused to do so, the urine was pressed into Kanchi's hand and scattered around her house, to 'purify' it according to Hindu custom.

It was a battle to the end. In December 1969 we received a note saying that Santa Kumari felt she was dying and would we come down and baptise her. We went down and found the dear old lady very perturbed in spirit and weak in body. How lovely it was to give her the comfort of the word. 'Believe on the

Lord Jesus Christ and you will be saved.' 'If you will confess with your mouth the Lord Jesus and believe in your heart that God raised him from the dead, you shall be saved.' She quietly testified to her faith, and then we prayed and were able to assure her of her acceptance by God. Her husband, the old witch doctor, sat by all the time. He didn't interrupt nor show any resentment when Hilda spoke to him.

As we do not baptise people ourselves, we sent to Tansen, and Pastor Attan came over at once. Santa Kumari had rallied a little but was still very poorly, so a delay was not advisable. It was clinic day in Pyersingh, so Attan went down to Paimey, where Santa Kumari lived, on his own. Next day Hilda and Pavitri went down and found the witch doctor declaring he would never allow his wife to be baptised. As he was very deaf, to carry on a conversation with him was not easy!

In the late evening Hilda and Pavitri returned to the dispensary to be ready for the next day's clinic, but Attan stayed. He had several meetings with the believers and several long talks with Santa Kumari's husband, but he refused to allow baptism. Eventually Attan called the believers together. His own comment, when he came up to tell us, was that he had never heard such simple, clear testimonies. But the cost of obedience, as several frankly admitted, was too great for them to face, and some feared that under pressure they might draw back. Two women and one man, however, were baptised, and a number of babies were dedicated.

Attan had to return to Tansen, and shortly after, Santa Kumari died. The believers were ready to give her a Christian burial, but her husband objected, and a battle raged over the corpse for most of the day. Eventually, believers and Hindus joined in carrying the body out on to the mountain and burying it there. There was no ceremony.

Her husband then said that unless his three sons performed the requisite Hindu ceremonies for their dead mother, he would take his own life. They stood firm until they found their father going off into the jungle with a rope to hang himself. They ran after him, brought him back and then capitulated, saying they had been under extreme pressure from the Christians. They then performed the Hindu ceremonies.

Led by Tez Bir, the witch doctor, all the neighbours then rose up against the Christians. A great meeting was called, and threats and abuse were hurled at the believers. The council imposed a fine of twenty-five rupees on each Christian, no small sum. One of them was fined another twenty-five rupees for selling his pig, because being a Christian pig it was considered unclean, and this was a great offence in the eyes of Hindus. As he was also forbidden to sell it to Christians, it was difficult to know what the poor man could do. The Christians refused to pay the fines, and to prevent a further battle one of Tez Bir's sons paid it all! The Christians were told they were not to come to Pyersingh for fellowship or allow us into their homes.

Amma refused to listen, and so the council got her eldest son to try to force her and her younger son to return to Hinduism. This nearly broke Amma's heart. With Santa Kumari her old friend gone, Amma got the idea she was going to die too, and that she would be given a non-Christian burial by her eldest son. So she set out to come to us, and arrived late one evening in a state of panic. We feared she would not live until morning. But she did—and is still alive at 103!

Tez Bir continued his anti-Christian campaign, and managed to keep his sons from attending church services. The daughters-in-law, however, were much stronger characters. A series of strange things happened. Gomaya, the one who had stood by Santa Kumari, got ill. She came to the dispensary complaining of stomach pains. Hilda treated her, but the pain persisted. We prayed with her, but she still didn't improve. Hilda sent her to Pokhara Hospital. The doctor there was an experienced Christian. She, too, could not make a diagnosis, but the symptoms made her feel she should operate. This she did, but she found nothing seriously wrong. Gomaya came back seemingly cured. Three weeks later she died.

Shortly afterwards, Tez Bir's second daughter-in-law died. We only heard about it after she had been buried. She had apparently gone out into the forest, complained of a headache and, to everyone's amazement, died. Some months later, to our horror, the other daughter-in-law also died. We realised that there must have been a lot of witchcraft going on, for Tez Bir had said he was going to get his whole family under his domination, and these three had been keen Christians.

Tez Bir's son-in-law was the first man to be baptised in Paimey. So Tez Bir brought in a Brahmin to make him a Hindu again and purify his home from Christian defilement. The son-in-law tried to withstand them. He said he had Christ in his heart and not all the Brahmins in the world could get him out of there. He went on to say he didn't want the services of the Brahmin, nor did he believe in this purification, nor would he pay for the ceremony. In spite of this the Brahmin went ahead and did his part; this consisted of chanting various spells and sprinkling a concoction of cow dung and urine around. He finished by telling the council he had felt ashamed to do it in the face of such courage.

Not one person who took a stand for Christ in those early years escaped being summoned by the village elders. Pavitri herself was called before the whole village and commanded to renounce Christ. We were down in the dispensary at the time, and could see across to the other side of the village where the crowds had gathered. We heard afterwards that they applied every pressure they knew to make Pavitri give up her faith. She stood firm, but the council members went on and on, until an old man got up and said, 'You might as well give up. I've seen it; when these Christians are real, even if you threaten to kill them they won't give up. And if you do kill them you will be worse off, because ten more will come in their place.' So they let her go.

In December 1968 a big meeting was held in Paimey. Five Christian men were called by the village elders in front of about 300 to 400 people, and asked if they were Christians. When they said they were, they were warned that their houses would be pulled down around their ears if they continued to meet for Christian worship. One man, Narhu, who eventually became our pastor, was taken into custody for two days, during which time he was given no food and his Bible was taken away. He was then released and sent home to bring all his fellow Christians. He didn't do this. Later the council forbade anyone to help him with his land. As everyone relies on help from his neighbours to plant and reap their fields, this made things very difficult for him. However, he just went on quietly, and gradually his neighbours, ignoring the council's orders, came back to help him.

Three of the men said they would not come for services and they stopped their wives from coming as well. One, however, told her husband they could do what they liked to her, she was going to the service. Her husband eventually became a pastor!

Another believer was forbidden to allow any Christians to enter his house, which adjoined his parents' house. His father threatened to disinherit him. Tension grew and another big meeting was called. At the meeting the father said that unless his son promised to perform the Hindu rites for him at his death, he must at once leave his home and no longer consider himself a member of his own family. These rites were very important as they ensure that a person passes into the next life. It shows great lack of love and concern for your parents if you do not do them.

But this man and his wife refused to forsake Christ, and so were disinherited and cursed and told to leave at once with their four children. They moved out into a buffalo shed. One day, after his wife had cooked the evening meal for the four children, dirt was thrown into the food, and she was struck on the face with a stone.

Soon after this we sent the father, Churia, into Tansen to get medicine and supplies for us, and we told our Norwegian friend there what had happened. She asked Churia, 'How are things in Paimey?' and got the reply that everything was all right. She said, 'But I understand a family has been turned out of their home for following Christ.'

'Yes,' came the reply, 'that's us, but everything is all right.'

We didn't know until years later that during this period, to avoid arrest, Churia was going out at 5.00 am each morning and not coming back until 10.00 pm.

At the same time as this was happening, we went down to Paimey and twenty-five people joined us in Amma's house for evening worship. The Nepali men took the lead. There appeared to be no spirit of fear. The singing went on until after 10.00 pm.

Meanwhile we were having our own problems with the dispensary. We had been hindered in building a new dispensary in Pyersingh because we had refused to be involved in what appeared to us to be dishonest ventures. Furthermore, relatives who had lived for twenty years in India had now appeared and wanted to lay claim to the land on which we were living. We had long sessions with them, and it was not easy even for Pavitri to understand everything. The man who had sold us the land seemed to be for us, but the others were full of greed.

It was not always easy for us to remember that we didn't fight against human beings, but against the wicked spiritual forces in the heavenly world, the rulers, authorities and cosmic powers of this dark age. We were in the midst of a spiritual battle.

13

Stress, Change and Illness

We were not aware of it at the time, but this uncertainty over our land rights, as well as other factors, were beginning to loosen us from Pyersingh. The problem was that the owners of the land were saying that we could never have the freehold of the land. We had trusted the man who had let us have it originally, but now it seemed that others could lay claim to it. Until we knew definitely that it couldn't be taken away at a moment's notice, we were hesitant to put up any further buildings on it.

We had been going up and down to Paimey regularly because it was Pavitri's home village and most of the believers lived there. At the time that Amma had been baptised, Pavitri's older sister, Diddi, and her husband, Narhu, were also baptised. Diddi had become a Christian first. After she believed she underwent a real trial of faith. She and Narhu were childless, and because of this his relatives had pressed him to take another wife. (It is very important to a Nepali man that he have a son to carry out the proper rituals at his death.) The fact that his wife had become a Christian made his relatives even more vociferous on the subject. He resisted as long as he could, but in the end he yielded and took another wife. They all lived together in their one-room house–the two wives and Narhu. You can imagine the stress!

Diddi's state of mind was made even worse when Narhu had a daughter by the second wife. Talking about it later, Diddi said she used to cry to God every day when she was out cutting grass for the goats. She asked him to do something. She used to escape alone to the forest and go down on her knees and plead with God to hear her cry. God did do something: her husband became a Christian.

Now what to do? Should he turn out his second wife and keep the first? Should he make a settlement on his first wife and live with the second? He, too, started to pray for an answer to their predicament. This is not a unique problem for new Christians in areas where polygamy has been practised. With some exceptions, it is against the law for Nepalis to have more than one wife, but the law is rarely enforced. Narhu wanted to follow the Bible and be 'the husband of one wife'. But he felt he couldn't turn either of his wives out or refuse to live with them.

Then, in a sad but amazing way, Narhu's answer came. His baby daughter died. Shortly afterwards, the baby's mother went off with another man. He was free. In the eyes of Hindus, when one partner deserts the other the marriage is annulled. It seemed that God had his hand and eye on Narhu, for when the group of believers decided to choose a pastor from among themselves, they chose him. Narhu was a suitable choice for pastor. Most of the believers belonged to the Magar tribe. Within the tribe there were higher and lower subgroups, and Narhu was a Rana, which was the highest subgroup. Thus he was a natural leader by birth.

The pastor and the main body of believers lived in Paimey. There was also a man there who had been a captain in the Indian Army. He had been responsible for getting a school established in Paimey. Being an enterprising man, he asked us to start a dispensary there.

At first we declined, as we felt we had enough work in Pyersingh–and we certainly did. Paimey was a two-hour walk up and down two very steep hills. It was true we were already going back and forth because of the church there, and whenever a medical emergency occurred among the believers we would immediately go. But the captain kept on at us until we gave in and agreed to come down for a weekly clinic. He cleared the school office for us, and we held the clinic there each week. It was the beginning.

Pavitri, her younger sister Saili, and pastor Narhu and his wife bought land in a section of Paimey known as Chargallia. We needed somewhere to stay when we were down there, so we decided to build a small house on part of the family land. The house was to be built of mud and stone with a roof made of wood, felt and tar. Hilda had seen this type of roof used on pig sheds in Ireland, and for some reason thought it would be suitable for us.

Hilda and I went to Kathmandu to pick up the materials for the roof; the wood had already been cut to the measurements we had planned. The house would be started when we returned. Hilda had other business to do, so I duly arrived back alone with the roof. It was no easy task to transport the stuff from Kathmandu up to Paimey. I had to arrange for porters to carry it all up on their backs–loads of plywood, felt, gravel and tar.

When I got back I found that the building had already been started. There was no way that the roof was going to fit it. What to do? Too much had been done for the building to be pulled down. The rainy season was coming; we had to put some sort of roof on it. We had no tin or other alternative. Thatch was the only answer, and that was in short supply. With great difficulty we at last managed to find some thatch, and the house had a roof.

This meant that we had a spare roof. What could we do with it? The clinics in Paimey, meanwhile, had grown beyond capacity, and we were being pressed to build a dispensary there. Land had been found for it next to the family land in Chargallia. So we thought it might be a good idea to build a dispensary which would fit the roof we had. But none of the Nepalis felt they could tackle it.

Not long after this I went to a mission conference in Kathmandu. There I met an engineer friend of mine. He asked about the work in Pyersingh and Paimey, and I lightheartedly said, 'I suppose you wouldn't want to come and build a dispensary to fit the roof we have, would you?' To my utter amazement, he said he would love to come. He thought he could leave the work in Tansen in the charge of his Nepali workers. He would have to ask permission of the mission director, but he would let me know.

I was therefore surprised the next day when a man I only knew by sight came up and introduced himself as Bob Buckner. 'You don't know me, but I am coming to build your dispensary.' It transpired that my engineer friend was needed in Tansen after all. However, it was felt that building the dispensary in Paimey was an ideal assignment for Bob. He had been having problems with learning the language, partly because he was working in places where people wanted to practise their English. At that time I was the only English-speaking person in the whole Paimey area. Anyway, I was going to be in Pyersingh and he in Paimey. So if he wanted to get anything done and survive, he would have to speak in Nepali!

He was God's gift to us. He was more suitable for the job than my engineer friend. He was a practical man, ready to work alongside the Nepalis rather than just direct them. He made us a lovely dispensary which fitted the roof perfectly. So we now had two dispensaries to run.

When we were in Paimey we lived upstairs in the 'thatched-roof' house, and Saili, Pavitri's sister, lived downstairs. It was just one room up and one room down. Pavitri stayed in Pyersingh.

About that time, our Interserve chairman and his wife came to visit us. Before they came we thought we should get a toilet built. We asked one of the Nepali men to do it. We pointed out the place where he should dig the hole, back around the side of the house. Our toilets were nothing superior, being only a hole in the ground with bamboo matting round them for privacy. We then went up to the dispensary in Pyersingh.

We only came down again a few hours before the arrival of our guests. They were to stay upstairs in the thatched house. It had a verandah with a superb view of the Annapurna range. Whenever we had guests we ourselves went up and slept on the floor of the new dispensary.

As we came down the hill towards the house, we stopped still in our tracks. There was the toilet. It had been built all right. There it stood, in all its glory, plumb in the middle of the view between the verandah and the Annapurna mountains. We were horrified.

However, there was nothing we could do. We asked the man why he had built it there. He said that the ground was too hard where we had suggested; it was nice and soft and easy to dig where he had put it. The view? No, he hadn't thought of the view. After all, you could go anywhere and see the mountains.

Not for the first time I realised that we and the Nepalis see things from different perspectives. They have now got used to the fact that these crazy foreigners want to stand and look at the mountains, climb them, and take photographs of them. They have now put this to good effect to encourage tourism, of course. As far as the village Nepalis are concerned, however, the mountains had always been there and always will be, so what is there to get so excited about?

Our visitors arrived and were shown to their room with a view. To make matters worse, only a bamboo mat had been put around the hole. It was not very high, so when you stood up your head poked over the bamboo matting. The chairman got his wife to take a picture of him in the loo. He later showed it to his friends with the caption: 'The view from our hotel in Nepal.'

In 1972 Hilda felt that she should go home to retire. Pavitri didn't feel she could run the dispensary, though as I have said, she was excellent with midwifery cases. I told the village councils in Pyersingh and Paimey that I was not qualified to run the dispensaries. They begged me to stay, saying that they were not interested in qualifications but in results, and that I was better than a witch doctor. They said people recovered with my treatment. I felt it would be traumatic enough for the Nepalis to lose Hilda without my going too, so I stayed.

I went to Kathmandu to see Hilda off. In the evening after she left, we had a mission meeting in the house of one of my friends. She was called away to a maternity case, so I was left to host the meeting. It was a long meeting, with reports and much discussion. By the end of it I was physically and emotionally exhausted. It had been a trying day. It had not been easy to see Hilda off after working with her for so many years.

The trials of the day had not ended. As I was about to walk back to where I was staying, two officials from my mission came up and told me that the mission wouldn't allow me to stay in Paimey to work on my own. I felt they might have chosen a better moment to tell me, and I told them so in no uncertain terms. The situation in Paimey had been known for some time, yet no discussion had ever taken place about the future. They had put me in a very difficult position. What's more, the mission officials left the next day, and there was no opportunity to discuss the matter further.

I had to return to Paimey. Pavitri was surprised that I had come back alone. She and the other Nepalis couldn't understand this, because they knew there were many doctors and nurses in Tansen, Pokhara and Kathmandu, and thought one could have been spared to help. When I further explained that I had been told to leave, Pavitri stared at me in disbelief. Her reaction was: 'Do people cease to be Christian when they become Mission?' It wasn't the first time I found it difficult to explain mission policy to village Nepalis.

I didn't know what to do. It was the beginning of

the rainy season, the most difficult time of the year. Patients couldn't get out for medical care; they could only come to us. During part of the time, the river became too high to cross and there was no way they could get to the hospital in Pokhara. At that time it was a twenty-six-mile walk over very difficult terrain. Pavitri begged me not to leave her alone with such heavy medical responsibilities.

A little later I received the official mission letter saying I must go home. I could see the mission's point of view. They were taking their responsibility for me seriously. I was 'alone'—though it angered the Nepalis when they heard people say that. I was manifestly not qualified for the work I was doing. The old image of the pioneer missionary spinster going it alone was a thing of the past; it must not be allowed to continue. I was faced with a dilemma. The mission folk could see things with more objectivity than I could; they were not plunged in the midst of human need, knowing people might die if not treated. If I left I would leave my Nepali friends without help. If I stayed I would be disobeying the mission. I didn't know what to do. I took the mission letter into my room, got down on my knees, and spread it before the Lord and asked him what he wanted me to do.

I was in the habit of reading a daily devotional book called *Daily Light*. I read it this night. I had forgotten that it was the night of my special verse, May 20th. I read: 'Jesus said unto her, "Mary. Fear not, for I have redeemed you. I have called you by name, you are mine. The sheep hear His voice. He calleth His own sheep by name. The sheep follow Him for they know His voice." '

The next morning's readings contained these

words: 'My grace is sufficient for you, for my strength is made perfect in weakness. I can do all things through Christ who strengthens me. We have this treasure in earthen vessels that the excellency of the power may be of God and not of us.'

I was also reading Frederick Mitchell's book, *At Break of Day*, which is a commentary on the *Daily Light* portions. He wrote: 'When we are feeling weak and insufficient, then is the time for faith to triumph over feelings and say that we can do all things through Christ who strengthens us, and in that confidence to assume the God-appointed task which is indeed beyond us, and to wrestle with the problem or the foe because He is with us. It is God's wisdom that the treasure should be in weak earthen vessels lest due attention should be called to the vessel, when the treasure is that which is important. So let us rejoice and be glad in spite of all human frailty, for strength comes in our joy, and the Lord's joy and the Lord's strength are sufficient to stand any strain which may be imposed or permitted by our understanding God.'

I had a letter from Hilda urging me not to leave Pavitri. I went over to Tansen to consult with my friends and the leaders there. They all agreed I should stay, and promised that a doctor would come out once a month for two or three days.

So I wrote to the mission asking permission to stay on at least another three months to cover the rainy season. I told them that I realised that it is more difficult to be responsible for missionary personnel because they bring God's will into the situation, often feeling they have a hot line to him. I quoted the passages I'd been given. I also said that it had come into my mind that Frederick Mitchell had changed his plans and had died in a plane crash going home. I was to remember these words. However, the mission did agree to allow me to stay.

I went home in September. I had not been feeling well for several months. I had a medical examination when I went to Tansen and was pronounced fit; my condition was put down to the stressful circumstances under which I was living. However, I was worried about myself. I had a haemoglobin count of forty-one per cent. I had lost nearly three stone in weight and was a very bad colour.

Soon after I got home I was to go to Canada with Hilda to visit her brother and our prayer partners there. But first I went for a holiday in Sidmouth with my aunt. While there, my feet began to swell. I didn't say anything to my aunt. When I got to my room I looked at my body and my swollen feet. I was as thin as a rake. I had been feeling for some time that I had cancer, and now I was sure of it. I was in a real panic.

As usual that night I had a quiet time of prayer and Bible reading. I poured out my fears to God. I was reading an Old Testament passage, 1 Samuel 30:18, when out of the page, as it were, jumped three words: 'David recovered all.' Completely out of context as they were, God took these words and made them live for me. I felt him put his hand on my shoulder and say, 'Mary, you will recover all.'

I had an appointment booked with the doctor at Mildmay Mission Hospital before Hilda and I went to Canada. When the doctor saw me, I was admitted to the hospital immediately. I was given several pints of blood. I was told I had a large lump inside me and I needed an exploratory operation. Again, I was in a panic. I had been the medical social worker at

Mildmay. I remembered two missionaries who had come in while I was there. They had both had laparotomies and were found to have inoperable cancer—it had just been a case of opening them up and then closing them again. The more I thought about it, the more I thought that I, too, had inoperable cancer. I remembered how weak I had felt, the non-responding haemoglobin, the condition of my body. How foolish I had been to stay that extra three months in Paimey. If I had come earlier I might have been in time. How pig-headed I was.

Then, amazingly, I found in my locker the letter setting out the reasons why I had felt it right to delay my home leave. How it got there I will never know. I had no idea I still had it or had brought it into the hospital. When I saw that letter, it was as if God said, 'Don't panic, Mary. I was in your staying. You will recover all.'

However, I was still jangling all over and could get no peace. My friends, Hilda, Pam and Doris, had given me a card on which were the names of God. One, Jehovah Shalom, means, 'The Lord send peace.' As I looked at it, I said, 'Lord, that is just what you will have to do for me, as I have no peace anywhere.' Peace did not suddenly come, but over the next few days before the operation I was conscious of a new serenity and trust. I knew that many people were praying for me.

On the afternoon before my operation, a friend from Nepal came to visit another patient in the ward. Hearing that I was in the ward, she came over to me. I was pleased to see her and told her how glad I was that she had come to see the other patient. 'She is in a panic,' I said. She had overheard the doctors talking about someone who had a tumour and thought it was her. Later I used to tease her and say, 'You had the rumour and I had the tumour!'

My Nepal friend looked at me and said, 'Well, you are not in a panic; you look so calm and peaceful.' How I praised him for the outward evidence of what he had already done in my heart!

I had the operation and a large mass was removed from my caecum. I had to wait about two weeks for the result of the biopsy. As soon as the doctors came into the room, I knew what the result was. The surgeon came to my bed and said the biopsy result had shown that they had removed a malignant tumour. They hoped that it was encapsulated. He looked straight at me and said, 'Is that all right?' I simply said, 'Yes.' What else could one say? I remember being slightly amused at the time, even under the circumstances. I have often smiled at this since.

And it has been all right! I did recover all. And when God does things, he does them abundantly. I am now over thirteen stone.

14

We're Back

As my medical prognosis was not certain, I had to remain in England for a year. So that I would have a western companion, Hilda came back with me to Nepal. We left a year to the day after my operation. As we returned, two verses from Psalm 78 were special to us: 'He led them on safely' (verse 53), and 'He guided them by the skillfulness of his hands' (verse 72).

We stayed with friends in Delhi and Kathmandu on the way. Because of delayed arrivals and roads blocked by landslides, we wondered whether we would get to our appointed meeting place with our carriers on time. To our great joy we did.

The weather was good, but the recent rains had left a very slippery and muddy trail, so we were unable to make much speed. We had to stop on the trail when nightfall came, and all we could find was a distinctly public and not very dry verandah. It was, however, more welcome to us than any five-star hotel. We felt how privileged we were when, before we went to sleep, one of the Nepali men (now a pastor of a newly built church) led us in prayer. He thanked God for our return, and for God's presence and protection over them during our absence. We lay looking up at the stars and listening to the sound of the jungle; both of us were so glad to be back in our beloved land of hills and valleys.

Next day we made an early start after only a cup of tea—there was not much food in the village. We pressed on, leaving the men with the loads to come on at their own pace. We arrived earlier than Pavitri and Saili had expected. There were no phones to let anyone know one's time of arrival. People were usually expected within a day or two of the planned dates; we had arrived on the right day anyway.

Owing to the heavy monsoon, the place was somewhat of a shambles. However, Pavitri and Saili had whitewashed the cottage and put in a lot of effort to make it habitable. One of the ways village Nepalis welcome you is to 'lipnu' the floors and verandahs. To 'lipnu' means to spread wet mud over the existing mud floor and then to make it smooth and welcoming. Unfortunately for us, dear Pavitri and Saili had been hard pressed, and had started the mudding too late. So it was difficult to find a dry spot on which to put anything.

Hilda's bed had been made and was ready to sleep in. Mine was still piled high with things that had been taken off the floor so it could dry. I contemplated sleeping on the floor on a straw mat but it was still too wet. The oil lamps all needed cleaning and fresh oil put in them. By the time that had been done it was too dark to clear the bed. We also had to go and fix the water pipe before we could get enough water to fill a kerosene tin and have sufficient for a good wash. In the end Hilda and I shared the single bed, since there was no other clear dry space for sleeping.

However, the discomfort was nothing compared to our delight to be home. Both of us had faced the possibility of never seeing our Nepali friends again. We were so thankful for the way Pavitri and Saili, in spite of great difficulties, had kept things going during my illness. Our hearts did fail us a little, as we realised what a job we would have to repair, remake and tidy up the place. The white ants had eaten books and even a desk and wardrobe. Some of the clothes I had left had gone mouldy—a common thing to happen during the rainy season.

We missed the electric lights of English homes, not to mention hot and cold running water. Hilda particularly missed her long, hot baths. Now she had to make do with a kerosene tin of water heated up over a wood fire. That in itself was a luxury. We did not miss a washing machine, as we had never owned one in England and so washing by hand was no change for us.

I remember asking in Kathmandu if I could do some washing. The hostess at the guest house said, 'You can use the washing machine.' I apologetically said, 'I'm sorry, I don't know how it works.' One of the new young people, overhearing me, said, 'No, it's so old fashioned, isn't it? I don't know how to work it either.' Is this what is called the 'generation gap'?

On our first Sunday we were thrilled when twenty-two joined us for the worship service. Pastor Narhu led, and showed clear gifts of leadership. We looked at the group, some new to us, and wondered afresh at the gospel we have to preach; so precious is it that these folk had been willing to give up all they had for it. Truly we felt we were among those 'of whom the world is not worthy'.

The need for the medical work was as great as ever. We wondered how we were going to run both dispensaries. Neither of the village councils were willing for us to try to get Nepalis to take over. It is mission policy that we hand over to Nepalis as soon as possible, but often Nepalis mistrust their own people. In fact, I have heard Nepalis say, when they were forced into leadership positions, that they were the victims of the mission's 'Nepalisation' policy.

The mission chairman and his wife, for whom we built the loo, came for the dedication of the dispensary site in Paimey. The message the chairman gave steadied and helped us. Speaking from John 6, he drew our attention to the inadequacy of the supply, yet the Lord accepted what was offered. In John 6:6, we are told, 'He Himself knew what he would do.' He had the plan and at the right time there was enough to meet the need. We were to prove that.

We were continually under stress. In Pyersingh three beams in the dispensary rotted and the building was in danger of collapsing. The goat stable was unsafe, so we moved most of the goats down to Paimey. They had to be led down there. They had never been out before. Saili went down to Paimey to receive them, Pavitri and Hilda acted as escorts, and I stayed to 'hold the fort' in Pyersingh. We had a very steep hill at the back of the dispensary in Pyersingh; to get to Paimey we first had to go over that hill. Hilda, who took one of the older and larger goats, related how they were both out of breath and puffing when they reached the top. A Nepali woman, resting her load, looked at them both and pointing a finger at each in turn said, 'Old woman, old goat.'

We were glad of the new building in Paimey. It was certainly drier than the one in Pyersingh, especially in the rains. The monsoon period, from June to October, is always a time of difficulty. I am quite sarcastic to people at home who close their prayer meetings in August. If they think their prayer meetings make no difference to us, they might as well close down all the year. We needed their prayers even more during this period. It tends to be an anti-social time, when the damp atmosphere eats into your spirit. Hilda thought the incessant rain even depressed the hens, as we got few eggs.

Journeys in Nepal during the monsoon can be hazardous and difficult. It is nothing for the torrential rain to sweep away bridges on the main motor routes. There are hazards on the road too. The bus may have to stop at one side of a fresh landslide, and then you have to get off the bus, wade the river or make a wide diversion, climbing dangerously over shifting mud to get to the other side and catch another bus there. It is often a quarter of a mile or more away; tricky enough without luggage, but positively dangerous with it.

We used to get cut off and were unable to get supplies in during the rains as the rivers were too high. If we had not had any mail or supplies for over a month, two of the Nepali men would attempt the journey. It was often very difficult for them and, of course, impossible for us. We tried to keep enough supplies on hand, but storage was a problem, and we usually ended up providing for rats and insects, who were also hungry.

The Nepalis in our area used to live mainly on millet which they made into porridge and bread. We found the porridge almost impossible to eat, but we did eat a sort of flapjack bread they made. It was quite nice when it came freshly out of the pan. I enjoyed it, but Hilda used to say it tasted rather like a linseed poultice. I used to wonder when she had eaten one! The bread was dark brown and could be indigestible when cold, rather like chewing through an old-fashioned gramophone record—though I have never tried that either.

In Pyersingh we lived in what was known as a leech garden. I thought that was one of the reasons why we were offered the land. In fact, when we eventually moved to Paimey, people said to me, 'Well of course you couldn't stay in that leech-infested place, could you?' They implied that was ample reason for leaving.

In the rains we were plagued with leeches. I once had seventy-eight on me by the time I got to the top of the hill behind us. If I had stopped to take them off, more would have climbed on while I was stationary. So I used to go as fast as I could to the top and pull them off on a bit of land that didn't have leeches. The leeches may be small to start with, but they quickly become bloated with your blood, often reaching over an inch in length. We had a tin outside the dispensary with a sign on it saying, 'Put your leeches here.' We had a solution in the tin which killed them. Otherwise, if people just picked them off, we would get hundreds more.

We had our joys as well as our trials. One Sunday we went to the hamlet where the child greeted our friends who were lost with 'Jaya Masih'. Due to landslides, leeches and a very slippery road, it took us over three hours to get there. We were thrilled to find over twenty adults and ten or more children gathered there. We were greatly encouraged by the spiritual depth of those asking for baptism. It was wonderful to see God planting his church through those whom the world would count as 'foolish'.

This group eventually moved down to the 'terai'—

the flat land along the border with India. One of them became their pastor. They were persecuted for being Christians and for sticking to their faith. Two of the group were taken into police custody and were made to crawl on their hands and knees in the hot sun. One had his guitar and the other his Bible tied on their backs. They were beaten and made to crawl up and down outside the police station in front of a big crowd. The police tried to make them recant and deny their faith. The police continued to beat them and make them crawl up and down until their knees and elbows were bleeding. Both men, however, remained radiant in spirit and showed no bitterness, only joy at the privilege of suffering for Christ.

I visited the men with a friend last year. My friend was impressed by the number of times we were down on our knees praying. Everything, it seemed, was prayed over. The prayer times were not forced or burdensome but simply the outworking of a living relationship with a loving, heavenly Father.

The missionary who built the dispensary, Bob Buckner, used to come to visit us from Pokhara where he was working. He was so strong and quick he could reach Paimey in a few hours after his regular working day had finished.

One New Year's Day he and his wife, Hazel, arrived with their son, David. David was doing a project on Hinduism in Nepal for an American university where he was a student. He wanted to stay with a Hindu family. It was difficult to find a family who would take a raw, young American at short notice. He didn't want to have anything to do with the Christians. He felt that we had spoiled the Nepalese culture. But he had taken no account of those who had lived among the people and learned their language and therefore knew what the people themselves felt. It is true that we carry with us our concepts of civilisation and our westernised Christianity. However, the message of the gospel itself, as it is found in the Bible, is good news in any culture.

At first David had to settle for a compromise and stay with a man who was a Christian but whose wife was a Hindu. At the time there was also, for a short period, an American Peace Corps volunteer in that village. After a few days we managed to persuade one of the local Hindu headmen to take David in. He had been a captain in the army, so he had had some contact with the West.

David had a rather romantic idea of Hinduism, as taught in America. I knew he would find it difficult to live entirely as part of the family, so I urged him to take a jar of coffee with him as a change from the rather monotonous village food. He refused, as he wanted to live as they lived. It sounds admirable to live like the local people, but it is possible only for short periods, and I can count on the fingers of one hand the people who have come to do this and have succeeded over any length of time. They themselves said they were not sure how much more they accomplished by doing this. Making relationships is really an attitude of heart, not conforming to outward circumstances. Pavitri used to be rather scornful about our dressing as they did. She would say to me, 'You don't walk like a Nepali, and whatever you do you will still look and walk and act like an English person. The important thing is that you love us. And we'll know if you love us.'

So David went off to his project of living in a

proper Hindu family. He did not want to come to our services. He was determined to explore on his own the wonders of Hinduism.

After about ten days he arrived at our door. He asked me if I thought the first family would take him back. He had been rather scornful about them, so I was surprised. 'What's happened?' I asked.

'Well the Hindu family give me my meals separately, they won't let me eat with them. The man has three or four wives and several children.' By local standards he was rich and the home comfortable. However, by western standards there were few comforts. But David was not seeking these anyway. He said, 'They treat me like an outcaste.'

'Well,' I replied, 'in their view you are. Even though you would not call yourself a Christian, the mere fact you are an American makes you a cow-eater, and therefore it is not right or fit that you should eat with people to whom the cow is sacred.' I got the feeling he was slightly disillusioned with being immersed in real Hinduism. He also seemed a bit lonely. The Christian man took him back as part of his family. David came to see us when he was ill, and at other times. No longer did he scorn my jar of coffee. And whenever he heard I had just baked a cake, he did not hesitate to stay.

Since David was in the area, Bob also visited us. One day he announced that he was going to build us a house in Paimey in his spare time. 'You have had enough of sleeping on the dispensary floor when visitors come,' he said. His plan was to assemble all the doors and windows in Pokhara, using wood they had there so as not to denude our hillside. A Nepali man, Kancha, from the mission's technical school in Butwal, would come and supervise the local men who would do the building. He said it would cost about £350. We had enough for this in the account. There was a piece of land on which we could build. It was a terrific undertaking as all the supplies had to be brought on a truck to Dulegaunda, twenty-five kilometres from Pokhara, stored there, and then carried up the hill by porters.

Kancha, the man from Butwal, was to live with the pastor. I remember worrying about whether they would get on all right. They did; in fact, the pastor's wife treated him like the son she never had. How often we worry uselessly.

Hilda and I were to have several sleepless nights, however, wondering if we should stop the project altogether. Bob sent cement to make the building earthquake-proof. It became apparent it was going to cost over £1,000; where were we going to get the money? Perhaps we hadn't sat down and counted the cost. We sent some of the cement back. However, we eventually came to the conclusion that we should go ahead and trust that the money would come. But we didn't feel we should ask for it.

We had enough money to cover the first stage: paying the workmen. However, because of some new international regulations, we could not actually get the money given for the work transferred from England. Bob, being an American, said he could lend us the money, but we didn't want to do that if at all possible. It was a great relief to us when the cheque was finally cleared; the man sent in to collect the money arrived back at noon on the day we had to pay the men. I can still remember the man walking in with the load of supplies on his back, and our joy and relief when we knew he had the money with him.

We still had to pay for all the roofing, doors, and windows that had been made in Pokhara, and this came to over £700. What to do? Then something happened which seemed to us a miracle. Hilda had a letter to say that someone in Ireland had died and left a legacy for the work in Pyersingh and Paimey. It was big enough to cover the bill! We have never had a legacy before or since. Now the only outstanding bill was for £250 to cover Kancha's wages and the supplies from Butwal.

Then I had a letter from the General Secretary of Interserve to say that my church had sent an unusually large gift for me and he thought I might like some of it for the work. I wrote saying we were building a house and would be grateful if they could assist us. I did not state any amount. When my letter arrived the General Secretary was away, but a friend of mine was in the office. She looked up my church's giving and the overall support I was receiving. (We had to raise from churches and friends enough to cover our support each year.) To my joy she wrote, 'After looking at the support you are getting, I feel we should send you £250.' Hallelujah!

Hilda had now been back with me for over two years. I was getting good medical reports. Her sisters needed her, so she felt she should go home. The day she had arranged to go home turned out to be only two days after the house was completed.

The day of the dedication of the house saw us still putting on finishing touches. We were hanging curtains and David was putting latches on the windows when we saw, from the upstairs window, our guests arriving–they were on the path only ten minutes' walk away. We had invited fifty Nepali folk from nearby, and twelve westerners who had to do the eight-hour trek up. We only had four beds, so the rest had to sleep on the floor.

Narhu planned the Nepali service. We all marched around the house singing. We then went to the big living room for the English service taken by an American, the Rev. Park Johnson. We sang 'Great is Thy Faithfulness'. Then we went around again, different people saying prayers in each room. The special verse of the day was from Exodus 15:17–'You shall bring them in and plant them in the mountain of Your inheritance, in the place, O Lord, which You have made for You to dwell in.'

Our Christian Nepalis told us that the Hindus had tried to put the skull of a child in the walls of the house so that our spiritual power would be limited. The Christians had thrown it out. I realise that the sceptical West will find this hard to believe. I have no doubt that when the devil or his agents are entrenched in a building or in a person, we will not be free in the building, nor will that person be free. We need to come against this evil power directly and command it to go in the name of Jesus. There is no other way.

Two days after the dedication, Hilda went home to retire properly. I was left to run the two dispensaries. I had a lovely new house in which to live. It was such a treat to be able to shut real doors and windows. In Pyersingh we only had plastic ones.

As I had no medical training, running the dispensary was quite a scary experience. it wasn't just a first-aid post; it was more like a small rural hospital where everything imaginable came. At first when I saw a great crowd of people carrying in a patient, I would be petrified. I never knew whether it would be someone with acute intestinal pain, or someone who had fallen out of a tree, or a mother six days in labour or you name it. Whatever the case, I would be expected to deal with it.

It was amazing what God did for me. As the years went by I could go and face whatever it was without fear. I used to look around sometimes and say, 'God, where is the fear I should have? I'm trusting you that whatever case comes, you will help me to cope with it.' No one was available from the mission to help me. Pavitri worked in the dispensary, as well as being in charge of the maternity work. I, likewise, helped her with that.

It was good for my Nepali. I only spoke English to God and my dog, Yeti. Yeti would walk into the dispensary and I would say something like, 'Yeti, what are you doing here?' The patients would often ask, 'Does he understand English?' I would reply, 'Yes, he's very intelligent. He understands three languages: Magar, Nepali and English.'

15

Help! Where's the Doctor?

Over the years we had many stressful medical moments. Our nearest hospital in Pokhara was a twenty-six-mile walk away. (In later years, after the Pokhara to Kathmandu road was built, it was sixteen miles to the road, and then a fifteen-mile bus ride to the hospital.) From time to time we received medical help of various kinds; certainly any visitor with medical qualifications was roped in to help us.

I remember a maternity patient being carried in who had a retained placenta. I was on my own, as Pavitri was away. A nurse who came to visit arrived earlier than expected. I immediately took her into the dispensary, and only after she had successfully removed the placenta did I allow her to have a much-needed cup of coffee. Placentas did not always come out quickly. As patients had to be carried such long distances, they often didn't come until some days after delivery.

One particular lady lived a five-hour walk from the dispensary. After four days in labour, she had had a dead baby at home. The family waited another three days and when the placenta had still not come they brought her to us. She was a high-caste lady and her husband was an important man in the village. It was a matter of prestige, therefore, as well as the need for carriers, that the husband brought fifteen men along—

though only one woman. So we had to cope with them all, as well as the patient. Fortunately Pavitri was with me. Though Pavitri had had no formal training, she had become expert at abnormal deliveries which, of course, were the only kind we had. Nepalis believe that having a baby after marriage is a perfectly normal and natural occurrence and make nothing of normal childbirth. They only seek help when things go wrong. And even when things go wrong, they will first call the witch doctor, or they will wait and wait, hoping that things will work out by themselves. After all, it is very expensive to get people to carry your wife for specialised help, and the average village Nepali can't afford it.

However, expense was not the problem with this lady. Considering what she had been through, she wasn't in too bad a condition when she got to us. I was having a severe attack of gastroenteritis myself and was hardly able to stand, but I went to help Pavitri. We tried to get the placenta out, but it wouldn't come. I went outside and told the men that they would have to take the patient to the hospital in Pokhara. They talked with one another and then said they couldn't go to Pokhara. In spite of much discussion they remained adamant: thus far had they come, and no further would they go.

I asked Pavitri to explain the seriousness of the position to the two women in the hope that they might be able to make the men do something. Pavitri and the other woman talked to the patient, but her answer was, 'I have had enough.' One could sympathise with her; it was now a week since she had first started labour, and she had been pulled about by us and had had all sorts of other methods used on her in the village before she got to us. She went on to say. 'I am not going to hospital. Either you get it out here, or I'll die, but no further will I go.' We realised that they all meant this, and that they would only take her home to await whatever might happen. She had had enough, and we were beginning to feel we had too.

Pavitri and I looked at each other in despair. Then the words of Psalm 34:6 came to me: 'This poor man cried and the Lord delivered him out of all his distress.' Turning this into a heart-felt prayer, I said, 'Lord, there are three poor women here; we cry to you to deliver us out of our distress.' Pavitri and I then went to work again, crying to the Lord to undertake, strengthen and enable us. Within a short time the placenta came out. Within the hour the patient was on her way home, where she made an uneventful recovery. Everyone was mystified why we couldn't have done it before.

Besides maternity cases we often had accident cases. One of the nastiest occurred when two men in a village had a fight. The villagers rushed down to tell us that one seriously injured man was on the way. Hearing of his condition, we advised them not to bring him to us but to go straight to hospital. However, they didn't do so. About half an hour later a large party of men arrived carrying the man. He was in a very bad state and would obviously need to go to hospital. As it would be a police case, Pavitri was anxious that they should go as soon as possible. If the patient died, we would not be able to get rid of the body, or the accompanying friends, until the investigation of the case was over—and that could take over a week!

I went into the dispensary to write a letter to the hospital. The man was in a blanket hammock outside, ready to be carried to Pokhara. Suddenly he sat up and asked his friends for a drink of water, which they gave him. He lay down and a few minutes later there was a mighty wail. Three of the men who were with him had hysterics as he had relapsed into unconsciousness and appeared dead. I tried to quieten his friends and went to the patient. He certainly looked dead; I tried to find his non-existent pulse. I knelt beside him and laid my hands on him and prayed that he would recover consciousness. To everyone's amazement—mine included—he sat up and asked me to treat him. I explained that there was nothing we could do and that we were getting him to the hospital as quickly as possible. He thanked me and lay down again. We pressed his friends to get moving with him. They set off down the hill. At the foot of the steep path from the dispensary, about a ten-minutes' walk, there is a small temple. There the man again asked his friends for a drink. They put him down and gave him a drink. He drank it, and then apparently died immediately, for within a minute we heard the death wail again.

We felt so sad for them, but realised the goodness of God to us. We had been saved from being involved in a police case. I didn't understand the full ramifications of this, but Pavitri did, and felt that God had worked a miracle for us.

It was difficult to make the decision as to whether to send a patient to the hospital or not, and the issues were often not understood by the patient. Hilda once had two men who came because they had chopped off the top of a finger when cutting grass. Both had rushed to the dispensary, bringing with them the cut-off piece of finger. Hilda was able to sew one back on successfully, but she had to send the other one to the hospital. Later they sat together on the dispensary verandah discussing their cases. The one who had gone to the hospital found it difficult to understand why he had to pay a large bill when his friend had had his finger sewn up for next to nothing by Hilda.

Pogi, a local village girl, the manure man's daughter, was told by a gynaecologist who was visiting us that she must go to the hospital for her first baby. We were all primed to send her as soon as she went into labour. She duly arrived at the dispensary, we prayed for her, gave her two hundred rupees to help with her expenses, and sent her off to the hospital in Pokhara. The next day in a crowded dispensary, with the rain coming down outside, we remarked how fortunate it was that Pogi had gone the day before to Pokhara when the weather was good. Then a man burst through the back door of the dispensary and said, 'What can I do for my wife? She has retention of urine.'

It took us some time to grasp the fact that this was Pogi's husband. 'What has happened?' we gasped. 'Where is she?'

'Oh, she is just over there on the path; we didn't go yesterday.'

What could we do but bring her into the dispensary, rely on God, and do our best in spite of the fact that the gynaecologist had said there was no way that Pogi could have the baby normally? Thankfully, at that time Val Collett, a trained nurse and midwife, was with me. I carried on with the other patients, praying hard all the time, and with Val's skill and God's help, Pogi had her first baby daughter.

Believe it or not, two years later another specialist said that Pogi had to go to the hospital for the birth of her second baby. We were told when to send Pogi, and that the baby would have to be induced. Pogi came, was prayed for, given some financial help and sent off again. Four days later I heard that Pogi was back. I asked whether she had had a son or a daughter. I was told she had not had a baby, but she had seen the King of Nepal! She had never been to Pokhara before and she really enjoyed the visit. What about the baby I asked? There had been no bed in the hospital, so she went and stayed with friends. They told her that the King was coming, so she went to see him. She saw everything else in Pokhara too. All this took two or three days, and as the baby hadn't come, she decided to walk home.

When I saw her I tried to persuade her to go back to Pokhara, but she thought it was too long a walk in her condition, and she didn't want to be carried. On Friday Pavitri went away. I urged her to come back quickly. Sunday night Pavitri was not back, and Pogi went into labour. Knowing that I was no good with maternity cases, her youngest brother decided to read the Bible instead of calling me in the middle of the night. He found James 5:14, which says: 'Is any among you sick, let them call for the elders of the church.' So they sent for the pastor, who went down and prayed with Pogi. At 5 am, as Pogi was rolling around in pain, they called for me. I went down to her house and found that the baby was not coming immediately. I asked them to bring Pogi to the dispensary. By this time Pogi was crying, 'Get it out, get it out!' I was praying, 'Lord, keep it in until Pavitri comes.'

By 6.30 am other patients began showing up at the dispensary. Pogi, who had by that time also arrived, was still crying, 'Get it out!' It didn't appear to be too imminent, so I got on with the other patients. At about 9 am Pavitri arrived back, but said that she would not help and that Pogi should go to the hospital. I knew she wouldn't go, but I sympathised with Pavitri who, like me, was afraid of what might happen or not happen. Pavitri's nephew, Man Bahadur, who had been helping from time to time in the dispensary, arrived about that time as he thought I might need help. He couldn't come before because he had had to cut grass for Pavitri's buffalo and goats while she was away.

By this time I was near the end of my tether. Pavitri was refusing to help, Pogi and her family were refusing to go to Pokhara, and there were about thirty other patients waiting. I said to Man Bahadur that we had better pray. I prayed quite a mild prayer, but Man Bahadur obviously thought the situation required more drastic measures. So he prayed, 'God, please get that devil out of Pavitri and bring her here immediately! Amen.' Well, within ten minutes Pavitri arrived and within the hour Pogi had her second daughter with no trouble at all. Then we went on and saw the rest of the patients.

Over the years I had several emergency crises with Pavitri's health. One time I had given her all the medication I could and her fever was still up to 105°F. She often had malaria and responded to treatment, but this time nothing would bring her temperature down. I had a visitor staying with me and, like the Apostle Peter with his mother-in-law, we got down on our knees and rebuked the fever. The fever left Pavitri and did not return.

Another time she had been very sick for several weeks—so ill that both she and Amma thought she was going to die. In fact, Pavitri got her mattress taken out of her room and put on the ground outside. This was often done in Nepal when people were likely to die. Unless one knew this, the statistics at our mission hospitals and dispensaries might be misleading (often true of statistics). In the early days hardly any patients died in the hospital. This was not due to the skill of the doctors or nurses, but rather to this custom of removing the very sick patients from their hospital bed and putting them on the ground outside; people had to die on mother earth. The relatives would take this action if they or the doctor thought the patient was about to die. Thus most patients were 'discharged' prior to death.

Amma was very distraught and sat pummelling Pavitri's feet, crying that since she was not eating she must be dying. Pavitri, who was not getting any better, refused to take any more medicine or to go to hospital. I was in despair as to what to do. I went down to the dispensary to pray, and asked God what I should do for Pavitri. He seemed to say, 'Give her an antihistamine.' I didn't think we had any. But I looked in the dispensary and found we had a sample of Benedryl that someone had sent us. I read up about it, and it seemed that if this drug didn't agree with the patient, the after-effects could be worse than the illness itself. I decided that if Pavitri was willing to take it, I would give it. To my surprise she agreed to take it.

At this point a large party from a nearby village arrived, carrying a hysterical woman who had been bitten by a snake. I left Pavitri to take the tablet and went down to deal with this other patient. It took me well over an hour to cope with them all. When people carried anyone into the dispensary, they usually decided that it was their opportunity to have all their

aches and pains seen to as well. After I had calmed the
snake-bitten patient, dealt with the others and sent
them all home, I went up to see Pavitri. To my amazement she was sitting up eating an egg. I started to cry.
Pavitri stopped eating, looked at me and said,
'Shouldn't I be eating an egg?' She didn't look back,
and over the years Benedryl became her cure for all
ills.

A maternity case I will never forget was Sheti,
Pavitri's niece. She called for us at about 5 pm one
pouring-wet Sunday evening in the middle of the
rainy season. When we got to her house she was in
labour and bleeding heavily. Pavitri examined her and
decided she must go to the hospital. We told her
father, but we all realised, looking at the weather, that
it was going to be impossible to take her. Carrying a
patient in Sheti's condition over the slippery paths
would be very difficult, and the river might be so
swollen that it would not be possible to carry her
across.

We were inside Sheti's parents' small, mud-and-
thatch house. Sheti was on a straw mat by the fire.
Pavitri and I were kneeling on the mud floor, our
bottoms almost in the fire. We looked at each other,
realising on a human level that we couldn't face seeing
Sheti bleed to death. Pavitri was panic-stricken and so
was I. There were pools of blood; we tried to do what
we could. Then suddenly we were both conscious of a
Presence with us. God said that we were not to worry;
he was in charge. And we proved this to be true.
Pavitri worked skillfully, and a baby girl was safely
born. We made certain the baby was all right and then
turned our attention to Sheti, who was still bleeding.

I had given the baby to Sheti's mother and told her

to wash her. She said, 'Me wash her? I've never washed a baby. My mother always washed them.' Sheti's mother had seven children. So I said, 'You are Sheti's mother, and now you're a grandmother; it's your turn to wash the baby.'

Both the mother and baby survived. Within the year we again had to fight for the baby's life during a most awful bout of diarrhoea. We tried everything and nothing seemed to help. The grandparents on the father's side were Hindus, and since the baby didn't improve they said they would take her to the witch doctor. On that Sunday, the baby was prayed for in the church service. After the service I asked God, 'Is there anything else we should do?' He seemed to suggest a drug I had not tried before. I went round to the house and gave it to her. The baby quickly recovered.

We often had emergencies with babies. One of the Christians rushed into the dispensary one day during a busy clinic with a moribund little girl in her arms. The child had suddenly collapsed, and the neighbours had told the mother she was dead and there was no point in taking her anywhere. The mother, however, not heeding them, had gathered the girl up in her arms and had run all the way to the dispensary. I was on my own that day. The girl was not dead, but neither was she very alive. After I had prayed for the child, I gave her some medicine and suggested that the mother stay with her sister-in-law near us for the rest of the day. When I went down to see her at midday, the child was asleep and seemed a bit better. I didn't have time to see her again until evening, and she was sitting up, seemingly quite well.

On the way home, the mother met her husband.

He had come in from his work in the fields and had been told by the neighbours to go and collect the body of his child from the dispensary. Imagine his delight when he rounded the corner and met his wife and little girl, who was holding out her arms to him.

Another time, I was just closing the dispensary when the local witch doctor's wife rushed in with her seemingly moribund son. Her husband had been treating him. As he was getting worse rather than better, she told her husband she had no faith in him and was bringing their son to me. This child, too, was jumping around the next day, after prayer and medicine. He always regarded me as his doctor after that, and the mother never again had faith in her husband's treatment. I had another witch doctor's wife who always came to me; in fact, her husband used to send her because he was never able to cure her.

Prayer and medicine were never far apart in the dispensary. Even in the mission hospitals the doctors and nurses would often have to deal with things they had never seen before. After obstetric cases, the worst for us were the many accident cases: people cutting themselves instead of grass, chopping their feet instead of wood, husking their fingers instead of rice, falling out of trees when cutting leaves, and falling down hillsides while grazing their animals. And during Dasai, an annual Hindu festival, even getting flung from a ping, the Himalayan 'ferris wheel'.

One late evening a man was carried in, having slipped on one of the hillside paths and rolled many feet down the side of the mountain. Others had slipped there and gone down to their death. This man was severely injured and had a badly broken leg. He was unconscious. We could do nothing more than make him comfortable for the night. It was a warm, sunny evening, so the friends decided to sleep with the patient in the outpatient waiting shed. However, about midnight it began to rain, so we had to move the whole party into the dispensary. We advised them to make an early start to the hospital next day. In the morning, however, he and his relatives were still in the middle of the dispensary floor when the clinic patients started to arrive. During the long summer days they would often arrive by 5 am. I was grateful Val was with me because she was able to make the man comfortable for the long journey to Pokhara while I got on with the other patients. Everyone was pleased, as the man had recovered consciousness in the night.

Pandemonium reigned while the man's relatives and friends sorted out who would go and who would stay. They would be away for several days and their farms and animals had to be looked after. Fortunately, the family was not poor, so they could pay for the man to be carried. Poor families get into debt trying to raise money for transporting patients to the hospital. As the patient was conscious and feeling much better, they set off in high hopes of his recovery. We were sad therefore to hear, about a week later, that he had died during the operation on his leg. It wasn't the first time. We wondered whether it might have been better not to have sent the patient.

I found it particularly difficult to get foreign bodies out of various parts of people's anatomies. I remember a boy who limped in one day, having run a piece of corn stalk into his calf. There seemed to be no trace of it. I put on a dressing and told him to come back the next day. I was going away the day after and I knew he would never go to hospital. So I had to get whatever was in his leg out when he came back. I asked God to show me where it was. As I bent over his leg, to my utter amazement, the piece of corn stalk rose up in the leg, rather like a punt pole raising out of the water. I was able to get hold of it with a pair of forceps and pull it out.

Clinics were busy. One day I had 113 patients, a buffalo, a goat and some hens. It was a relief when some local men later went for training in veterinary work. One from our village was proclaimed their best trainee.

Pavitri was speaking one Sunday on Psalm 18:33— 'He maketh my feet like hinds' feet.' She said how difficult it was for me on wet trails, and she wondered how I would manage, because they were particularly bad that year. 'But,' she said, 'God has given her hinds' feet.' She went on to verse 29: 'By my God have I leaped over a wall.' She said, 'It was like leaping over a wall for Mary to take over the medical work after Hilda went home; but how wonderfully he has enabled her to leap.'

I would not be allowed to practise medicine here in England, and I know I couldn't do it. The choices are too great, the facilities too many, the man-made pressures too much. In the hills of Nepal, however, I daily faced 'life and death' issues. The fact that God was my first and greatest resource made it possible. I had assumed that anyone could diagnose as I did, but several doctors told me that God had given me a special gift of diagnosis. Certainly, I was conscious of God's help each day. I was also helped and encouraged by the expectations and great faith of the Nepalis.

One of our local Christians once brought a relative to the dispensary. The relative had been turned out of her home by her husband because she just sat and stared like a zombie. When I lifted her arm, it remained in whatever position I put it until I moved it again. When she came I happened to have a doctor visiting, and he examined her and said she was a hopeless case. It was an incurable condition, and I should not waste my time as she would never get better. I told this to her relative, who was a member of our local Christian congregation. She was scornful; what did the doctor know? She had brought her to the dispensary for God to cure her. Surely if we co-operated with God, she said, he would do the necessary. After all, he was the God of the impossible; didn't we believe that? I rather weakly agreed that we did. I also repeated what the doctor had said. This was pooh-poohed, and the request was made that we should get to prayer at once. So I prayed with her and gave her some medicine. Her friend also prayed and exhorted her to repent and believe on the Lord Jesus.

This patient was brought regularly every month for nearly a year. After a time she began to smile, and each time she responded a little more. I shall never forget when she spoke. In the end, she was so well that her husband took her back. As far as I know, she never believed and we never got any thanks or payment from the husband for his wife's return to health and mental stability. The former I had hoped for, the latter I had not expected. Our faith in God's power was strengthened.

16

Well, God, If You Don't Do Something, Nothing Will Happen

When I was in Pyersingh and Paimey, I often found myself saying, 'God has never let me down.'

My faith in God was greatly helped by the attitude of the Nepalis to spiritual things. They are orientated from birth to expect the spirits, good or bad, to be involved in illness and health. When I have asked Hindus if I might enlist the help of the Great God who made us, I have never known a refusal. Patients were grateful that I was bringing a spiritual power into the situation. The Christians would feel that they had not had the full treatment if we didn't pray for them. If we did sometimes forget, they would remind us to do so. I find that westerners often say that this is just superstition on our and the Nepalis' part. The Nepalis feel, however, that God knows more about the situation than they do, so it is foolish not to enlist his help.

In Nepal there are some diseases that are supposed to be spiritually caused and therefore can only be spiritually cured. One of these was called 'aphno betha' (one's own disease). Its symptoms were rather like pneumonia. As it was thought to be spirit originated, the mothers would take their afflicted children to the witch doctor first. The children often got much worse, however, and we got used to having them arrive at the dispensary almost unconscious. When we enquired whether they had been to the witch doctor during the past twenty-four hours, they would often say no, fearing that we might not treat them if they admitted to this. On being reassured that this was not so, and that we needed to find out what treatment the child had received in order to know what medicine to give, they usually admitted that they had gone to the witch doctor. We treated the children with large doses of prayer and antibiotics—and we had a high cure rate. Gradually it became known that we could cure 'spiritual diseases', and so parents began to bring their 'aphno betha' cases to us.

It was particularly in maternity cases that we saw God's mercy to us. Isolated as we were, there was often no possibility of getting the patient to a hospital. Qualified people used to say that Pavitri and I were spared much anxiety by not knowing all the awful things that could happen. However, we knew enough to appreciate when we were in a tight corner. One tight corner was the case of a woman who had been bleeding for several days and was in labour, not a happy state to be in when the nearest hospital is a day away. Villagers had been pressing hot stones on her to try to bring out the baby. We were sure it was dead, but in the end a baby boy was born alive and well. Then our troubles really started. We not only had a river of blood but she was spurting blood too. We did 'everything in the book'—except our book only said to send the patient to a hospital! Both Pavitri and I were working and praying as hard as we could, but nothing would stop the bleeding. Then Pavitri saw that the patient had several charms round her neck that the witch doctors had put on her; they were caught up in her clothes so we had not noticed them before. Pavitri became angry and said, 'How can our God work when you have these on?' She commanded that the charms be cut off and thrown away, and the relatives did this. Immediately, the blood stopped spurting, and in a little while ceased. After two hours we sent her home. She came back a few days later, completely well.

The Bible says that 'we wrestle not against flesh and blood but against principalities and powers and the rulers of darkness of this world.' Pavitri and I both felt we had wrestled not only with 'principalities and powers' but with flesh and blood too.

There was such a lot to learn in this healing business. We found we needed to keep sensitive to what God was saying in each case. This was certainly true for me one Christmas when Pavitri was ill. On Christmas Eve she developed a high fever and lost consciousness for three hours. She had been ill for some time and I didn't know what was the matter with her. I gave her medicine but she didn't improve. She had refused to go to hospital, saying she was too ill to be carried twenty-six miles swinging in a hammock.

On Christmas Day we were to go to the Christmas celebrations, but we couldn't leave her. We seemed to be under a big black cloud for the whole day. She began to get worse and said she was going to die. I laid hands on her and prayed, but there was no improvement. I went to bed exceedingly worried about her. In the night I woke up and wondered what to do. I asked God to show me. At about 3 am I got the extraordinary feeling that God was telling me to go and throw away some goat horns I had seen on a piece of wood jutting out from the side of Pavitri's house. At the time I had wondered where they had come from and presumed that Pavitri's nephews had put them there. I thought I was going a bit stupid. I argued that it couldn't be God saying this to me, and I wondered what Pavitri and the boys would think if I threw them away. The thought persisted, and then, coupled with it, came another thought: 'Also throw away the silver temple medallion you have.' I had got this some years earlier, and had intended to give it away but had never done so. I said, 'Lord, I don't really know where this is, and you can't expect me to root around in my cases at this time of night.' However, I couldn't rest, and I finally said, 'Lord, if this is you, please go on speaking.' I went to sleep and then woke at 5 am with the feeling that God definitely wanted me to do something about the horns and the medallion. So I got up, searched in my case and found the medallion. I went down with it to Pavitri's house and took the horns off the wall. I then went to the gate and threw them and the medallion into the jungle, saying, 'In the name of Jesus Christ get out, stay out and go where Jesus sends you.'

I returned to my room feeling rather stupid. About an hour later I went down to see how Pavitri was. She sat up when I went into her room and said, 'I hear you got some cauliflower from Pokhara. Please may I have some?' She went through the day asking for one thing after another to eat. She quickly gained strength and was well within two days. I had a visitor staying with me at the time. She knew nothing of my night activities, but said at breakfast, 'Where has the oppression gone that we felt yesterday?' I was glad to tell her what had happened in the night.

During her period of unconsciousness, Pavitri had gone through a great darkness. She was sure an old witch doctor who lived in another village had cursed her. She had met him, and he had asked her for money to go to hospital. She didn't feel able to give him any money, and she was sure that it was because of this that he had cursed her. These witch doctors call on the powers of evil and so can use satanic power. Several times we have known patients who had been told by the witch doctor that they will die before a certain day, and for no apparent reason they do.

Some time later, Pavitri and I were talking about the activities of evil spirits and how to deal with them. I mentioned the time when I threw away the goat horns when she was ill. She then told me that her nephew had been sleeping on the verandah outside her room that night, when at about 3 am he had been roused by Pavitri—at a time when she was still in a coma-like state. She had raised her left hand and pointed to the wall and said, 'Singh, singh,' which in Nepali means horn. The horns were outside the wall to which she pointed. She couldn't have seen them or known they were there. Her nephew said, 'I knew the horns were there, but I was much too scared to go out and do anything about them in the middle of the night. The next morning I saw they were gone, but I was busy cutting grass for the goats and buffaloes and didn't think any more about it.'

A boy living near us had a heart condition and was coming to the dispensary for treatment. He was also starting to believe the Christian gospel. He was responding to treatment and we were feeling happy about him. Then one day we heard that he had died. On enquiring what had happened, we were told that the 'bokshi' had got him. There are certain evil spirits that customarily enter a particular object or animal. In this case, a spirit had entered a cat, and the cat had come and attacked the boy on the verandah of his house. On their return from their work in the fields, the parents had found the boy in a bad state, and on his body were marks where the cat had bitten him. In the night the boy died. All the Nepalis were sure that he had died as a result of being attacked by the evil spirit. They assured us that no one was blaming our treatment, since he had been getting better with our medicine.

Some time later we heard of another child in the same village who had died after being bitten by a cat. Shortly afterwards the mother of the child came to the dispensary; she had lost her only child. She came to ask us if we had any power that could stop the evil spirit from troubling her. She said that she could get no sleep because the evil spirit, with the cat in its arms, was going round and round her house. Could we do anything about it? We talked to her about Jesus and his power to protect us against all the power of the evil one. We asked if she was prepared for us to pray with her, and she was willing for this. So we prayed, Hilda laying hands on her and commanding the evil spirit in the name of Jesus to trouble her no more. She then spent the night with the pastor and his wife, and they had more prayer with her, as well as later at her house. She never had any more trouble from the evil spirit.

For a time she was sure that the Spirit who was with us was greater than the spirits she knew and feared. She attended Sunday church services for a time. Then, due to local pressure, she stopped. All who came to the Sunday services were persecuted by their neighbours. The Christians didn't invite people to the Sunday services, for if they did so those people would be marked by the non-believing community. The Christians would invite them to the midweek meetings instead, which were not so noticeable, and only when they felt that they really believed and were able to stand up to persecution did they suggest they came to the Sunday services.

After our 'cat' lady ceased coming to the services, a boy she had adopted married one of the Christian girls. The lady did all she could to hinder him from becoming a Christian. Some years later she became very ill. I had a nurse with me and we both thought she might have appendicitis. It was too wet to get her to hospital, so for several days we gave her night-and-day care in our house. Eventually we were able to send her to the hospital. She came back cured, and has been attending our services ever since, though she has not been baptised.

God was very real to the Nepalis in many ways, not only in health matters. I found it a privilege to live among them. In so many aspects of their lives they were open to God and could see him revealing himself in their lives.

Jyoti lived about five hours' walk from us. She tried to be a devout Hindu. She was sure that the Living God could be found somewhere. She was a widow, but poor as she was, she did all she could to find the truth and salvation. She went to many Hindu shrines and to a Hindu community near one of the sacred rivers where widows especially went. The priest there was supposed to be a holy god. She found the widows there washing his feet and serving him in every way. They urged Jyoti to join them and told her that the man was a god and was very holy. Jyoti soon realised that this was not so, and she came away disillusioned and wondering whether purity and truth could be found anywhere. In her heart, however, she was still longing and searching.

One day when she was out cutting grass for her goats, she fell out of a tree and hurt herself. She went to the local witch doctor, but got no better. Her sister-in-law, who had become a Christian, suggested that she should come to the dispensary. The sister-in-law brought her on a Sunday. The dispensary was closed, except for emergencies, but we saw Jyoti, and afterwards she came to the service. When talking about it later, Jyoti said that she knew she had come to the end of her search when she heard about Jesus Christ. After only a few weeks, I was amazed how much of the gospel she had absorbed. She was in her mid-forties, and illiterate. There was no schooling for girls when she was young. As I spoke of Jesus, I remember her saying, 'Yes, I know he died on the cross for my sins and he rose again. He is alive and now he is with me wherever I go.'

Every time we saw her she was growing spiritually. She asked to be baptised. Although she was poor, she always came with her gift and her tithe. She praised the Lord, and talked of the wonderful things he was doing for her.

She had three sons: one who was mentally handicapped, another who was slow in school, and a third who always had to be prodded to work. Her main prop and stay was her daughter, who also became a

Christian. Then, while I was away on leave, her daughter died. On my return, I asked Jyoti what had happened. It appeared that the daughter had only been ill for a short time, but had died having a vision of Jesus and talking about heaven.

As Jyoti's daughter had been a Christian, the Hindus would not touch the body. In the East you have to bury a corpse very quickly. Most of the church folk lived about five hours' walk away from Jyoti's home. The villagers all turned against Jyoti, and mocked her for trusting in what they described as the 'westerners' god'. They taunted her with what God had done to her in taking away her daughter; what sort of God was he to trust in? They pressed her to renounce her faith and return to Hinduism. Previously they had made her life very difficult in the village, forbidding her to go to the village water spring. She was isolated and alone. She knew that the pastor and the Christians were away at a conference; it was no use sending for them.

What to do? She decided to dig a grave for her daughter herself down by the river. She had to carry the body herself, because the Hindus would not let her sons help her, as they were not Christians. Her neighbours watched her with wonder and surprise. Later she showed me the grave by the river. She had said prayers herself as she buried her daughter. On their return from the conference, the Christians came and held a service too. I commiserated with her, saying how sad it was for her to lose her daughter. But she turned to me with a radiant face and said, 'Oh, isn't it wonderful? Jesus has taken her to be with himself!' When I think of Jyoti, I am ashamed of all the things I moan about.

Jyoti came regularly each month to the church services, staying overnight, since it was a ten-hour round trip. I never remember her coming empty handed; she was always praising the Lord. 'Hallelujah' was her favourite word. She usually had some faith-encouraging stories to tell us. Two such stories were about goats. She told of a high-caste Brahmin man who had come asking her to sell him one of her goats. Since Brahmins were the highest caste in the Hindu religion, women of Jyoti's caste held them in great esteem. He offered her a good price for the goat, and said he wanted to use it for a sacrifice. Jyoti made what money she had by selling her animals; she needed the money and wanted to sell him the goat. The only problem was that he had said he was going to sacrifice it at the Hindu temple. Now that she was a Christian, she felt she should not sell goats for this purpose. She voiced this to the Hindu man. He pressed her and said it was not her responsibility what he used the goat for; her conscience could remain clear. He would give her the money, take the goat, and what he did then was his business, not hers. After all, he might not have told her, and then she would not have worried. But that was the problem: he had told her. Her conscience was indeed troubling her. However, he went on pressing her to sell the animal. On the human level, it was difficult for a woman in her position to withstand the pressure of a high-ranking man such as this. At last he persuaded her that it was all right. So she sold him the goat, and the Brahmin put the halter around the goat's neck and led it away.

No sooner had he gone than Jyoti's conscience began to rebuke her. She should not have sold him the goat when she knew it was to be used for a Hindu sacrifice. She repented of what she had done, and stayed up all night praying. She prayed that the man would bring the goat back in the morning. This was an impossibility. I have never heard of a goat, once sold, being brought back to the owner. Jyoti's faith was that the goat would come back. In Matthew 9:29, it does say that 'according to your faith be it unto you'. In the morning, in walked the Brahmin man—leading the goat! He asked Jyoti if she would take it back. The priest had not turned up, so he could not sacrifice it. He didn't need it for any other purpose, so he had brought it back. She gave him his money and joyfully took the goat back. She was still rejoicing when she came in some time later to tell us.

Another of her goat stories happened after she had been visiting us. When she returned home, she found that four of her goats had died. She didn't know the reason, but she felt it was a bad witness to the Hindus around—which they were not slow to point out. As she couldn't read or write, she decided to take her Bible and lay it on top of the bodies of the four goats, which she laid side by side. She knelt down and prayed, 'God, you are the God of the living, not the dead. Please bring these goats back to life. As a witness to those around that you are the Living God, bring life back into these goats.' Then, as she described it later, 'first one raised its head, then another, and then another. They didn't jump around at once, but they did the next day, and one of them had a kid.' I, of course, being western, said, 'Were they really dead?' She looked at me, incredulous that I should doubt her word. She had dealt with goats all her life; wouldn't she know a dead goat when she saw one?

Jyoti could not read or write. Nonetheless, she gathered young people together to hear cassettes which she cranked out on a hand-operated player. She couldn't afford the price of batteries for a recorder. Through Gospel Recordings, she acquired the whole New Testament on tape. As soon as she finished her regular work, she would put on a cassette to hear more of the word of God. Not being able to read made her a more effective evangelist, because she always had an audience when she listened to those cassettes.

Jyoti had two more lovely answers to prayer. The first was when her older sister became a Christian. The sister, also a widow, lived in a village three hours' walk from Jyoti and about five hours' walk from us. There were no Christians anywhere near her village. She, too, must have been a spiritually hungry and prepared person; within a very short time of hearing the gospel, she became a believer.

When the people of her village realised that she was a convinced Christian, they started to persecute her. One of the Nepali Christians' favourite hymns was: 'I have decided to follow Jesus, no turning back.' She sent this message to us: 'I am being severely persecuted for my faith; I am not allowed to come to the services—but, no turning back. I will come as soon as I can.' It was several months before we saw her again. The villagers had threatened her with the loss of her land if she took a foreign religion and had forbidden her to drink at the village water spring. But she remained firm in her faith. She could not read or write, but God had strengthened her through visions and dreams. She knew that Jesus was alive. He was her Saviour and had died for her, and she was not going to give him up for anything. Jyoti was, of course, delighted at the stand she had taken.

The second wonderful answer to prayer concerned Jyoti's husband. He had been in the Indian Army. The regulations regarding pensions changed. It seemed that Jyoti, his widow, would be eligible for a pension. Her house, however, had been burnt down and all records of her husband's service had been destroyed in the fire. We put together what information we could about his service and wrote to the authorities on her behalf. They wrote back, saying that they could do nothing unless we could produce his regimental number. Jyoti had no record of it and no idea what it might have been. We explored all the avenues we could, but drew a blank. It seemed hopeless. Jyoti, however, did not give up. She had faith that God would find the number for her. We couldn't see how it was possible.

Some months later Jyoti met a friend of her husband. They talked about old times, and in the course of conversation he mentioned that he had bought one of her husband's medals when he had been short of money. Jyoti asked to see it, and there on the back was her husband's number. This time the authorities wrote back that they had traced her husband's records and they would let her know if she was entitled to a pension. In the end she got it. 'According to your faith be it unto you.'

Another 'according to your faith' prayer was answered for a lady whose son, at the age of eight, had gone with his uncle to the Gurkha Recruiting Centre near the Nepal border and had never been heard of since. The family had heard that the uncle had died, but there was no trace of their son. His mother never gave up and believed that he would return. It was a regular subject in her prayers. The rest of us wavered about the likelihood of his being found, but she persisted that he would be. One Saturday afternoon in the women's meeting, God seemed to give the absolute assurance that her son would turn up again.

I went home on leave. When I returned, I was walking back up the trail home and I saw three figures coming towards me; two of them looked familiar, but who was with them? Imagine my joy when they reached me and introduced me to the third figure, their long-lost son. I was so excited that, most unculturally, I hugged him. Was he surprised!

His side of the story was that after his uncle had died he had wandered off and drifted from place to place until some Nepalis took him up to Darjeeling in India. They had given him a home and he had gone to school. It was only when he had grown up that he began to wonder about his own home back in Nepal. He couldn't remember the name of the village he had come from. He knew it was in west Nepal. He also remembered that two westerners had run a dispensary in the area. So with this scanty information he had come back to Nepal. He eventually ended up in Pyersingh. By that time Hilda had gone home and I was running the dispensary in Paimey. I, too, was away in England, but some relatives in Pyersingh realised who he was and sent him to his own home. His mother, of course, was overjoyed. Sadly this home-coming was not all joy. It created problems with his brothers over the inheritance, because they had assumed that he was dead.

The Nepalis continually strengthened my faith. Bunti, together with her husband Man Bahadur, became a Christian, and as usual local pressure was

put on her. She was told that her land would be taken
and she would be sent to prison. One day she was
inside her house praying when three men came for
her. They demanded that she come out. She was asking the Lord to tell her what to say; but they kept
calling, so eventually she went out to them. She said,
'What sort of men are you to take advantage of a
defenceless woman like me and leave these four children without their mother? If you have anything to
say, come when my husband is here.' She told me
afterwards, 'They went away without a word.' At the
time her husband was working in India, but was
expected home for Christmas. In addition, her three-
year-old son was very ill. We prayed for him in the
church, and he became much better after passing nine
large worms! The men never came when her husband
was home to have an operation in Pokhara. The family
have never been troubled since.

When I was leaving to go home to England for the
last time, a friend gave me a bag she had woven for
me. She and her husband used to live in Paimey but
had moved and started another small church in their
new village. The police had stopped the church members from meeting, and she, her husband and four
others were reported regularly to the police each
month. As she gave me the bag, she said, 'Mary, don't
worry about us. Even if they kill us we will not go
back, for what else is there worth living for except
Jesus?' I am glad to say that with the new freedom in
Nepal, the sentences against them have been quashed.
They have built a church on land they bought with the
bail money they had paid and then recovered. They
praised God that they had proved the truth of the
promise in Romans 8:28–'All things work together for

good to them that love God, who are called according to his purpose.'

Another of my friends was in prison for being a communist. While he was there, God spoke to him and told him to read the Bible. He didn't know what this was, but he got hold of a copy and read it. He was convinced of its truth and became a Christian. He was just as earnest a Christian as he had been a communist. He witnessed to his new-found faith where he worked and they gave him the sack, and said they would make a case against him for being a Christian. He took the matter to the headquarters of the firm in which he was working. As his work record was good, they refused to sack him. However, they said that if his boss wanted to make a case against him for his Christianity, they could do nothing about it. His boss did make a case, and he was put in prison. He was so active a witness there that he was released with a warning not to talk to others about Jesus. Like Peter and John in Acts 4:18-19, he couldn't keep silent. Shortly after he had received this warning, I happened to be with him in a taxi in Pokhara. I heard him ask the taxi driver if he knew anything about Jesus. When the man said no, he proceeded to tell him all about him.

When I went to Nepal in 1957, I had some preconceived ideas about the way God would reveal himself to men. For spiritual growth, a 'quiet time'—reading the Bible and prayer each morning—was essential. I still think it is a very important thing for those of us who can read. It is, however, those who hunger and thirst after righteousness who will be filled. If there is that hunger, then God will find a way to meet it. I am thankful to God for the privilege of living for so many years among these wonderful hill Nepalis. They have not been brainwashed to believe that miracles ceased in Bible times. They have that simplicity of faith that sees miracles happen. I liked their directness. I was doing the Nepali Theological Education by Extension course with our pastor. In this course you cannot proceed to the next question until you have satisfactorily answered the preceding one. At one point in the course, we were given many theological reasons for believing that Jesus is alive today and for believing in the resurrection. To the question, 'How do you know that Jesus Christ is alive today?' the pastor gave this answer: 'Because Paul met Jesus on the Damascus road and I met him in Pyersingh.' It was not the required answer, but in the end it is the answer we all must surely give. 'You ask me how I know he lives—he lives within my heart.'

17

Spirits Versus Spirit

We had clinics of between fifty and 150 patients. Quite a few patients had been to the witch doctor before coming to us. This was because many of them believed that their condition was the work of malevolent spirits. Therefore, only witch doctors who knew the tactics of these spirits and how to overcome them could cure their diseases. The witch doctors would also try to placate the various gods on behalf of their patients by telling them to bring a chicken or a goat as an offering to the god. The idea behind this was that you gave blood to save your own blood.

If there appeared to be no obvious diagnosis for a patient's condition, I would ask, 'Do you think you have a "bokshi" [evil spirit]?' Often a look of relief would come over their face. 'Yes,' they would say, glad that I recognised there was a spiritual force behind their illness. When I asked if I might pray for the healing of their condition, they would always say yes. Many patients in Nepal said that their symptoms were relieved after prayer, and in most cases they were cured.

Witch doctors have their 'arts' passed on to them from generation to generation, and they are powerful in the work of evil spirits. They can also be cunning. So I had to learn to be a bit cunning myself. If a patient was very insistent on having an injection, I would sometimes ask, 'Did the witch doctor send you for one?' It was usually easy to tell when the injection was meant to be part of the witch doctor's treatment.

Nepalis can see spirits, good or bad. They recognised that there was a spiritual power with us. We were told that when we moved on to the hillside in Paimey the Hindus actually saw the evil spirits leave it. These spirits were reported to say that they could no longer live there, because the Spirit with us was greater than the spirit with them. I was told that one of the spirits was seen walking up and down in the river bed below us, wearing hob-nailed boots and saying that now he had nowhere to live!

Pavitri and Saili were scornful of Hilda and me because we couldn't see spirits. One day they asked us if we had seen what sounded like a Irish hobgoblin coming to our gate in the night. Hilda was Irish, so I thought she might have seen such things. When we said no, Pavitri said, 'No, of course you westerners wouldn't. The dog is more sensitive about these things than you two. Don't you remember he went out and barked last night, but came back almost at once? He knew it was a spirit he had heard and not a human being, so he could do nothing about it.' She went on to say, 'Saili and I saw it come right up to our gate, and when it realised that the power with us was too strong for it, it turned and went back down the hill.'

Hilda recalled an experience she had had some years earlier. The Nepalis had been telling her that every evening an evil spirit walked round her property. Hilda had not really believed this. Then one time she was awakened in the middle of the night by a most eerie moaning sound. She looked out of the window and in the bright moonlight saw a 'ball of light', a sort of 'presence' moving through the grass, causing it to bend as it walked. It was making a most strange, unearthly sound. Hilda said it was so spooky and unnerving she felt the hairs on the back of her neck stand up. When she told her Nepali colleagues about it the next morning, they said, 'That's what we've been trying to tell you for days.'

A country like Nepal, which was closed to the gospel of God until 1952, is a place where the devil manifests himself in the most blatant ways. Those of us from the West think that we have some knowledge of God when we go out, but most of us have very little understanding of the devil and his powers. We may not even believe in his existence.

I don't remember a Nepali who came to accept Jesus because of a sense of sin; this came later. Many, however, came to recognise in Jesus a power that was stronger than the evil spirits they knew. They called us the 'shut-eye party', because of our habit of praying; and they sometimes begged us not to pray, because they said when we closed our eyes we got in touch with a Power that they couldn't handle.

Rabindranath Maharaj, in his book *Death of a Guru*, told how he, a Hindu guru, proved that the name of Jesus was more powerful than any evil spirit. Reading the book, I was struck by one particular sentence. Speaking of his father, Rabindranath says, 'Nana had been heavily involved in Hindu occultism and was critical of those who merely philosophised about their religion without learning to use the supernatural forces.' This is surely what many of us from the West do with our Christianity. We never learn how the supernatural power that God has made available to us can be released in everyday life.

On the various mission stations in Nepal, there were those who became labelled 'charismatics'. I was not against them, but saw no reason to be particularly involved with them either. One day I was preparing for a Nepali Bible study group that I was taking on Acts 10. I read in verse 44 how 'the Holy Spirit fell on them', and in verse 46 how 'they heard them speak with tongues and magnify God'. I was surprised when I believed I heard God say to me, 'I am going to do that for you.' He seemed to say, 'I will baptise you with the Holy Spirit not many days from now.'

The events that happened next made me almost forget about it. In the United Mission to Nepal we had been grouped administratively by geographic area. I had been linked with the Tansen team, because originally I had been seconded from there to Pyersingh. They had always been very kind to me and I relied on them for support and fellowship. But then the administrative structure changed, and we were divided into departments according to our type of work.

I received a letter saying that I was no longer part of the Tansen team owing to these administrative changes. I was now seconded to myself, and only answerable to the Health Services Secretary. I was very fond of the person then in this position, but I also knew that he hated desk work and was out of the office as much as he could be. He was a born innovator and pioneer. I might as well have been under the 'man in the moon'. When I went home on leave some time later, I laughingly said to a friend as I went through Kathmandu, 'If he ever enquires about me, you might mention that I went home three months ago.'

After receiving the above-mentioned letter from the mission I went on holiday, and travelled via Tansen. I asked why I couldn't still be considered part of the hospital team there. The person in charge said, 'We had to decide who we'd be responsible for in case of illness, and now we won't have to take responsibility for you.' I saw their point: I was a forty-eight-mile walk away. I realised how much pressure there was on the people in Tansen, and that the one in charge probably had no idea of what effect her words had on me. No doubt I over-reacted, but I couldn't help it, I was feeling so isolated. It therefore meant a lot when one of my friends in Tansen said, 'Mary, I don't care what they say, if you get ill, just send a message and I will come at once.'

I went on my holiday to India, wondering how I was going to face the future. On my first day on holiday, the friend I was staying with asked me to sit in the garden with her. She said, 'I thought you might like to chat as you are now on your own in Pyersingh.' I could hardly believe my ears.

As we sat talking, God said to me, 'I could baptise you in the Spirit with this friend and none of your excuses would be valid.' I knew this was true. However, I didn't say anything, I needed more time to think.

A few days later, when we were out together in a rickshaw going to a garden centre, I broached the subject. Several years after my conversion I had come to a crisis in my spiritual life. I was going with a friend to a conference of the Japan Evangelistic Band. I didn't know anything about them, but thought I would hear about my friend's work in Japan. Thinking it was to be about missionary work in Japan, I was surprised to find the conference was about 'sanctification'. Passages quoted were from Ezekiel 36:23b, 25-27. As the weekend went on I felt God was cornering me.

On the last night the speaker said, 'Would anyone like to stay behind for prayer?'

I was determined I wasn't going to. I started to go out of the door. Dorothy Burton, whom I had known at Ridgelands Bible College, leaned across the person next to me and said, 'Mary, should you be going?'

'No,' I said.

'Will you stay?'

'No,' I said.

'Will you come and talk to me?' she then asked. I had great respect for her, so I said yes.

When we got to her room, I told her how cornered I felt by God's words in Ezekiel 36. She just said, 'It seems obvious what you have to do.'

So I knelt and asked the Holy Spirit to come in and take complete control of my life and sanctify me. To sanctify in the dictionary is to 'set apart for sacred use, to free from sin or evil, to make the means of holiness, to secure from violation'. So that was what I asked God to do for me.

Miss Burton gave me the verses from 1 Thessalonians 5:23-24—'The very God of peace sanctify you wholly and I pray your whole spirit and soul and body be preserved blameless unto the coming of our Lord Jesus Christ. Faithful is he who calls you who also will do it.'

What happened after that is another story, but to return to the present one, as we were in the rickshaw, I remembered my friend had also gone through a similar experience.

I asked her about it and then said, 'Would you not also say you were baptised in the Spirit?'

'Yes,' she replied.

'What's the difference?' I asked.

'Oh, they are quite different,' said she, as she went off to work.

God then started talking to me through Psalm 51, especially verse 10: 'Create in me a clean heart O God and renew a right spirit in me.' Also verse 12: 'Restore unto me the joy of your salvation and uphold me with your free Spirit.' It was his free Spirit that God promised me.

A few days later we had an opportunity to talk again. My friend asked, 'Do you think you should seek the baptism in the Spirit?'

I told her about the pressure God was putting on my spirit and how I felt he wanted me to seek this.

'May we lay hands on you and pray that you will receive?' she then said.

'Oh no,' I immediately replied.

She looked a little surprised but said nothing and as it was time for her to get on with her work the conversation ended.

Later, on my own, I examined why I had said 'no' so quickly. I realised I was afraid. I so needed to be accepted and to feel I belonged somewhere. But supposing these friends prayed and nothing happened, they might reject me too. I couldn't face that. As long as they did not test the Spirit by laying hands on me and praying, I felt safe.

God was merciful and again confirmed that he was going to baptise me in his Spirit. He said he would do this in my friend's bedroom with her present, before I left next Tuesday. The actual words were: 'in the house of the daughter of Zion.' My friend lived in a house called Zion Cottage. I asked if I could tell her, but God said no, he would bring it about. It seemed like an impasse, since it was most unlikely I'd be invited into her room. I began to feel I must be going peculiar.

During the next few days I kept saying to God, 'Forget the daughter of Zion and get on and fulfil your promise to me on our own.' However, the Bible seemed full of verses about Zion. I found that even 'the daughter of Zion' appeared in my reading an unusual number of times. I couldn't get away from it.

Part of me was glad, and part sorry, at what happened next, as it seemed to completely divert us from my baptism in the Spirit. Another woman missionary arrived with an Indian baby girl which she was going to leave with the community in which my friend lived. When she arrived it was obvious that she would find it very difficult to part with the baby. Her situation, not my baptism in the Spirit, was going to be our priority.

On Sunday evening we went to a local church where a convention was being held. To my amazement, the speaker's subject was 'The Baptism in the Spirit'; unusual for a first-night meeting. I remember thinking, 'If he makes an appeal, I will have to go forward,' but that was not what God had said to me. However, the meeting was very calm and orderly and we returned home at 8 pm.

The next evening my last night, my friend and I went round the garden collecting plants for me to take back to Nepal. We came to a house in the grounds called Peace Cottage.

'Shall we go in and talk?'

'No,' I said, 'let's go back to Zion,' thinking at least

we'd better be in the right place if God was going to work.

So back to Zion we went. All except one person had gone to the convention meetings, and she was sitting in the lounge. We sat down with her, and my friend tried to draw me on what God had been saying to me. It was amazing, I felt as if I was bound in chains and I just couldn't open up at all. For two hours we spoke of God's ways and about the past and how good God had been to us. Then, as it was nearly 8 pm, my friend suggested we prayed before the others got back.

I felt I should kneel down, so I did. I also had a special prayer burden for the visitor who had to leave the baby behind. I prayed for her, and then felt free to say quite simply, 'God, please fulfil your word and your promise to baptise me in your Spirit.'

My friend then said, 'May we lay hands on you?'

This time I felt quite free to say yes. What they prayed I don't remember. When I got up off my knees my friend was going towards the kitchen. As she went she said, 'You might like a time of quiet; go into my bedroom.'

I couldn't believe my ears but got up and went in. As I entered the room, it was as if the glory of the Lord filled the place; it was radiant with his presence. I fell down on my knees beside the bed and praised him. I felt his spirit flooding me, I was glowing all over. I asked him why I had not felt free in the sitting room. He said, 'I was binding you to the word I had spoken to you.' I then said, 'Well, to complete it my friend will have to come in here too. Can I call her?' But God said no.

In the meantime she had come out of the kitchen

and was in the sitting room. It was now nearly 9.30 pm. She got up, went to the door and, looking out, said, 'Whatever is keeping them, why are they so late back from the meeting?'

It was as if God and I laughed together as I thought, 'If you don't hurry up and come in here, God will wait for his promise to be fulfilled, even if they have to be at an all-night meeting and we get no supper.'

After a little while she did come in, saying, 'How are you getting on?'

I almost dragged her in, and pacing up and down I told her what God had been saying to me and how I felt glowing all over. She then simply said, 'Well, we'd better praise and thank God together that he has done what he promised.'

We did, and then we got up, hugged each other and—'toot, toot' went the horn outside and in rushed the others, apologising for being late.

Looking back I'm amazed and grateful that, in spite of my misgivings, the interruptions and diversions along the way, God fulfilled his word and promise. This he continued to do.

I left the next day feeling a strange 'glow' through my whole being. I know that this is my story and others will have different experiences. I have included this because I think there are certain principles at work from which we can all learn. Often, blessings do not come straight away, and we have to hold on in faith to God's promises. Then it is important that we not only trust, but also obey, and sometimes he cannot take us any further until we have obeyed.

I went back to a mission conference in Pokhara. I had several tests of my obedience to the Spirit there.

When I was giving a report on the work in Pyersingh, the Spirit told me to tell what God had been doing for me, which I did. The next night the speaker asked us to be completely free in the Spirit. He said that if we had anything to put right with a fellow missionary, to do so; if we had a word from the Lord, to say it; if we had a message in tongues, to give it, and to feel quite open and safe with each other. If we wanted to raise our hands in worship, we were to do so; if we didn't feel that raising our hands expressed our worship, we needn't do so, but we should be open with one another and be obedient to the Lord Jesus. He asked us to pray specially for two people who were sick, one a teenage girl named Sarah, who had rheumatoid arthritis and was with us, and the other a missionary in Kathmandu.

I was feeling full of praise and joy and felt almost as if I had the night off, since I had been obedient the night before! I didn't expect to have to do anything except just quietly worship the Lord. Then suddenly he started to say, 'Mary, go over and lay hands on Sarah.' I was horrified. I looked across the room to where Sarah was sitting. I would have to go right across in front of everyone to reach the other side of the semi-circle we were in. There were about 300 people at the conference. Looking across the circle I saw one or two charismatic types and I said, 'Lord, you could nudge one of them to do it; they are near her.' Nothing happened; in fact, nothing really happened in the meeting. The speaker closed that part of the session and we moved on to the Communion service. We were still sitting in our big semi-circle.

The director of the mission, who was an ordained man, celebrated the Communion. For me the bread tasted like coal and the wine like ink because of the pressure on my spirit. I thought that it couldn't be God, so I said, 'Go away, devil, in the name of Jesus.' The pressure persisted. I then tried another tack: 'God, think how embarrassing it will be for Sarah if I suddenly walk over to her. You wouldn't want her to be upset would you?' In the end I said, 'Well, God, if this is of you, give me the guts to stand up, and if I'm just a fool, please see that no harm comes to Sarah.'

When the Communion service finished, I stood up and said, 'Would you all be with me if I went over and laid hands on Sarah for her blessing?' There was a murmur of assent. I crossed the room and said to Sarah, who was sitting in a wheelchair, 'Sarah, do not be afraid. It is just that Jesus wants to bless you and your family.' I then put my hands on her head and simply said, 'The Lord bless you and keep you, the Lord lift up the light of his countenance upon you and give you his peace.'

As I finished speaking, something–as it were–broke in the group; people started praising and singing, and crying out for Sarah's healing. One doctor flung his arms round me and wept on my shoulder. As I stood there, I said, 'Lord, do you want me to go on and pray for Sarah's healing?'

'No, if I want to heal her, I have other servants through whom I can do that; you go and sit down.' I did.

As soon as the meeting was over, I rushed out and went up into a small room on my own and fell on my knees, and asked the Lord's forgiveness for what I had done. After a little while I came out of the room, and a friend was coming up the stairs. She pointed a finger at me and said, 'Don't let anyone tell you that you did the wrong thing.' Later the family testified that they had all been blessed, even though Sarah was not healed. She is still not healed.

A most beautiful thing for me happened at another conference some years later. I was sitting next to an American missionary, and I turned to her and remarked that it had been a very good conference. She said, 'Yes, but the best conference for me was when you laid hands on Sarah. I had come to that conference only just able to walk up the front steps and having just been told I would have to go home. After you prayed for Sarah, I was healed. I was able to walk out of the meeting and have had no trouble since.'

When I went home for retirement in 1989, she came to the airport to see me off, and she said, 'Thank you, Mary, for being obedient in that conference in 1977.' I thought how nearly I had not been obedient. I was reminded that God says the Holy Spirit is given to those who obey him.

'Trust and obey, for there's no other way to be happy in Jesus but to trust and obey.' That line has an eternal truth in it. I still find, even now, that it's difficult to obey what God says to me. The problem for most of us is being certain that it is God and not our own imagination. However, as we 'trust and obey', we should increasingly be able to recognise his voice, just as we recognise the voice of a well-known friend on the phone. The Apostle John wrote: 'He calls his own sheep by name...the sheep follow him for they know his voice.'

Some of you may be wondering, 'Did you speak in tongues when you were in your friend's room in India?' No, I didn't. However, God told me that I would when I next visited my friend and she laid hands on me on my arrival. I usually arrived late, so I said, 'God, there won't be time.' I wrote and told my friend I was coming, and shared with her what God had said to me. Amazingly, I arrived there early, the only time that ever happened. My friend didn't say anything, and I lost my nerve to ask her. So I came back, nothing having happened.

Over the next few months, I kept feeling the pressure to write and tell her that she should have laid hands on me when I visited her. But I felt I just couldn't do this. I kept saying to God, 'Forget her and just give me the gift. It's yours, not hers to give.' But again the 'daughter of Zion' kept coming up until I was tired of it. So in the end I wrote to her. No sooner had the letter gone than I spoke in tongues. It was as if God was holding me to be obedient to what he had said to me and to trust he had said it.

My friend was right about the baptism in the Spirit being different from the 'second blessing'. For me, the 'second blessing' was putting my whole life at the disposal of the Holy Spirit and receiving his blessing and seal on my new openness to him. The 'baptism' in the Spirit, on the other hand, was like being immersed in the Spirit. I 'lit up' inside and 'glowed' all over. I just wanted to praise the Lord and to feel him pouring his joy into me. These wonderful 'feelings' still flood over me, and I find myself lifted up in praise and adoration in all sorts of situations. I would not go back in any way to my Christian life as it was before. I do not feel superior. Many friends, whom I greatly respect, argue with me about the baptism in the Spirit for theological and other reasons. I am, however, personally very grateful to God for the new experience of himself that he gave me. Life has never been the same since.

This does not mean life was or is all joy and sunshine. Not long after this, God pointed out to me that he not only said he would baptise with the Holy Spirit but also with fire. He said this would happen to me. I didn't believe it. Then some time later, at a conference, I went (late) into a room where four or five of my friends were praying. I sat down by one, and she suddenly started to say, 'Do not fear the baptism of fire with which you are to be baptised.' She went on to say exactly what God had said to me. I had told no one.

I still didn't want to believe. I asked a friend who was at the prayer meeting, 'Did what Rut prayed have any meaning for you?'

'None at all,' she said. 'I couldn't think what she was talking about.' So I wrote to Rut to ask her if it was me. She wrote back: 'Of course it was you, and you know it.' There is a sense that what happened in the following years was so painful it was like having my skin burned with fire!

I have tried to find the theological meaning of being baptised with fire. I haven't got very far. But I know what it means in experience, and I think you will too if you accept that it is a baptism given by Jesus in the same way as he gives the baptism in the Holy Spirit. I am still conscious of its outworking in my life.

In his book *Tried By Fire*, F.B. Meyer writes about 'the trial of your faith being much more precious than gold that perisheth though it be tried with fire' (1 Pet 1:7). He writes: 'Trial here is compared to fire, that subtle element which is capable of inflicting such exquisite torture to our seared and agonised flesh, which cannot endure the least taint or remnant of impurity, but wraps its arms around objects committed to it with eager intensity to set them free and make them pure; which is careless of agony, if only its passionate yearning may be satisfied; which lays hold of things more material than itself, loosening their texture, snapping their fetters and bearing them upwards in its heaven aspiring energy. What better emblem could there be for God and for those trials which he permits or sends and in the heart of which he is to be found.'

We used to sing: 'Refining fire, go through my heart and purify the whole.' But when it comes to the crunch not many of us want this part of the deal.

One day I had a visit from the headman of Pyersingh and the local Police Inspector. The Police Inspector started by asking me to give him an injection. I enquired what injection. He said, 'One for tuberculosis.' He had the medicine with him. I asked who had diagnosed him as having TB and where he had got the medicine. He named a shop on the motor road that was selling medicines. I advised him to see a doctor and be properly examined. I said I would give him the injection now, and also a letter to the hospital. He agreed to this.

After he had had the injection, he said he wished to see my visa and to send a report on me to central government. I gave him my passport and he wrote down the particulars. He then said, 'You are not to give out any books. Some of the school boys have become Christians and are saying it is not necessary to worship idols; if you continue to give out books, some foolish people may be converted.' I replied that I thought all Nepalis had the freedom to read world literature since Nepal was a member of the United Nations. I had myself read books about Hinduism, Buddhism and Islam, but I was still a Christian. Reading a book couldn't make a true Christian; a change of heart was necessary.

The headman then said that I was to send anyone who asked for spiritual advice to him and the village council, and they would give a certificate to those to whom I could speak. I replied, 'If anyone came to me with cholera and I had the cure, I wouldn't ask them if I could give it; I'd just give it. In the same way, if anyone comes and asks if I have a remedy for sin and evil spirits, I must tell them about the risen Christ and the power of the Holy Spirit.'

The headman looked at me and said, 'Then to you it would be sin not to tell?'

'Yes,' I said. 'You know that I do not force Christianity onto people, but my good book says I have to be ready to give an answer for the faith that is in me. I said I always found that Hindus, being spiritual people themselves, respected me because I spoke with integrity about my faith.

The Police Inspector then said, 'You should tell those children who ask for your books that the police will kill them if they are found with a book.'

I looked at him and said, 'I am sorry, I cannot say that.'

The headman then said to the Police Inspector, 'It's no good saying things like that to her. Whatever we do to her she will not tell a lie. I have worked with these people and I know.'

The Police Inspector replied, 'I know everyone says they are good people.' With that parting remark, they left. Five minutes later a school boy came for a book, which I gave him.

After this encounter with the police, I was rather pleased with myself, and felt God had helped me as he has promised to do when we as Christians are called before the authorities. Over the years I have often been surprised at the Nepalis' reaction to such things, and so I was on this occasion when I told them about the Inspector and the headman coming. I thought I had been rather brave on my own, but they dismissed it, saying, 'Well, of course you had to stand your ground. The headman and Police Inspector were only doing their duty in coming to try to make you afraid and stop you from making others Christian. That is what they are paid for. They have done their job, you have done yours, and everyone is satisfied. You will probably hear no more about it.' But I did.

Several weeks later I was working in the dispensary, and looking through the window I saw the Police Inspector sitting in the queue. Then I saw a small boy arrive with books in his hand. The Police Inspector reached out and took them. I thought, 'Ah, this is me for the high jump.' I could hardly concentrate on the patients until the Police Inspector came in. He produced a letter from the doctor at the hospital. It said there was nothing wrong with him and he only needed some aspirin. He was relieved to know he didn't have TB. I gave him the tablets, and he departed amicably making no mention of the books.

I wondered why? I had not long to wait. The boy came in and handed me the books. I looked at them in amazement. One was the *London Illustrated* and the other was another secular magazine. Had the Police Inspector come earlier or later, he would have picked up a John's Gospel and a New Testament. It was not often I gave out two secular books and no spiritual one. I felt our times had been in his hands. But that was not the end of the story.

A few months later, the headman arrived. He said, 'You know that Police Inspector who came to cross-examine you? Well, he's dead. He died in his village. I don't know what caused his death.' I was so relieved that I had sent him to the hospital and not just given him injections. I got the impression from the headman that he felt our Spirit had 'donged' their spirit. It felt as if we won that round. I was never cross-examined again.

I found that God consistently protected me in this way over the years, especially when I was left in charge of the clinic. When I was in England once, a doctor from my home church asked me how it was for me when a patient died, seeing that I was unqualified. I thought for a moment and then, not realising how the remark could be taken, said, 'I don't remember anyone dying except when a doctor was visiting me.'

The next round I feel we lost, though I do not understand fully even now how or why. It happened during the time I was running between the two dispensaries in Pyersingh and Paimey. We felt we should change plans and have the bulk of the work in Paimey, and have a clinic just once a week in Pyersingh. Pavitri and Saili both moved to Paimey, Saili living in the one house, and Pavitri and Amma in another house we built. A Christian couple who had come into the district but had no home went to look after the property in Pyersingh. But then there was a period of near anarchy in the area. The headman who had come to see me lost his job, and the village authority moved

to another village. The Christian couple were unable
to protect themselves or our property, and everything
was looted. The couple didn't stay. We reluctantly
came to the conclusion that we must close the Pyersingh dispensary.

In Paimey, the government surveyors came to
measure the land. The headman and other village
leaders said the Christians would not be allowed to
own land. Six families plus Pavitri and Saili were
affected, and the dispensary and the house we had
built were involved. This was a real trial of faith for all
concerned. The land was not measured at first, but
later the surveyors did come and do so. However,
decisions made then were to have far-reaching effects,
which are still being faced and sorted out. As Proverbs
29:25 says, it seemed as if 'the fear of man, which
always brings a snare' entered into the transactions at
this point. Property and ownership of land have
always been and still are very difficult matters in
Nepal, as elsewhere.

The surveyor said that those with jungle land had
to cut down their trees, otherwise the land would
revert to the government. In view of the mass
deforestation in Nepal, this was an amazing misun-
derstanding of a law which was originally made to
preserve the forests by putting them under government protection!

That the witch doctors were interested in our
activities we had no doubt. It felt as if they were
flinging everything they knew at us. Among other
things, I suddenly became ill.

Each week I had been walking the two hours
between the two dispensaries. One day I walked up
the steep hill behind our house and then started down

the other side to Paimey. I was feeling far from well, so when I came to a stone resting place half way down the hill, I sat down on it. People built these resting places to gain merit. I suddenly felt very ill indeed, and unable to go on. I wondered whatever was the matter with me and what I should do. Then I heard a voice say, 'The devil is a murderer; resist him.' I couldn't believe my ears and thought it was very peculiar. I knew I had to do something as there was no one there to help me, and I had to get on to the other dispensary. So summoning up what strength I could, I claimed Christ's power over the devil and Christ's sovereignty over me. I then got up and started to walk down the hill, but I hardly knew how to put one foot in front of the other. I claimed the promise in Isaiah 40:31 that they 'that wait on the Lord shall renew their strength, they shall walk and not faint'.

I got to the other dispensary to find patients waiting and also members of the Bible class ready for a meeting. I looked to the Lord for his enabling, saw the patients and took the Bible class. I was speaking on the power that Jesus has over the devil. They were more than usually attentive, and one woman said to me, 'These are very amazing things you are telling us.'

After they had gone, I again felt very ill. I commanded the devil in the name of Jesus to get out, told him that he had no claim on me, the house or the hillside. I would feel well for a bit and then ill again. I remember walking round the house, proclaiming out loud Jesus' victory over all the power of Satan and telling him we belonged to Jesus, who won the victory over him on the cross. I placed myself under the protection of the blood of Christ.

This went on from Tuesday to Friday. When I got

back to Pyersingh, I was much better; and to my great
delight, two visitors arrived, one a doctor and the
other a nurse. I was able to tell them what had happened, which was a help. I was glad too of their help
with patients.

Just prior to all this, I had been asked into Pokhara
for meetings and fellowship, but because of the pressure of work had not gone. I felt now, however, that I
should accompany my friends to the meetings, even if
it was only to make sure I was not going 'odd' living
out in the hills. In Pokhara I stayed in a house with a
minister who had had a lot of experience of demonic
forces. I told him what had been happening to me. I
said I wondered if I was going a bit mad, but on
hearing all the details he said he believed that I had
had a satanic attack. He added that he marvelled I had
survived.

Being rather ashamed of what I was feeling, I did
not share these things with the Nepalis at the time.
Later, when I did, they too were sure that it was a
satanic attack I had experienced, and that the witch
doctor had cursed me, wishing me dead. I had seen
him walking round my house. I was interested that
afterwards he would not meet me, but would go off
the path when he saw me coming.

People believed the witch doctor put 'spells' on
them. A child of about twelve died in the next village
and was buried. The witch doctor went and dug up
the body and took the head and ground it to powder,
believing it would enhance his satanic power over
people. Pavitri found the remainder of the head when
she was out cutting grass and learned what had happened from the neighbours. You may remember that
they tried to put the skull of a baby in the house we

had built. In the mission compound in Pokhara, they found children's skulls shallowly buried in their grounds.

We had a real trial of faith when Pavitri's younger sister, Kanchi, became ill. It looked as if she was going to die. We went from church and anointed her with oil and prayed over her. She improved but then she began to relapse again. Pavitri suggested I should go and lay my hands on Kanchi and pray for God's protection for her. Her husband had had an argument with a relative who tried to claim some of his land without paying for it. Kanchi's husband had refused to give the land. So the man, a witch doctor, told him to go and plough it. The day he did this, Kanchi became ill. Three other men who had disputes with this witch doctor all died. Pavitri said he was very evil. I am thankful to say that Kanchi recovered.

Truly we are not fighting against human beings, but against the wicked spiritual forces in the heavenly world, the rulers, authorities and cosmic powers of this dark age. An old hymn says, 'Thou art in the midst of foes, watch and pray'—in the Spirit, against the spirits.

18

Visitors

According to western advertisements, we lived where you go to 'get away from it all'. We were pleased to see the many visitors who made the trek to us, and usually they were pleased too. They would often say, 'Oh, it's just like camping!'

We usually had visitors during Christmas. Each year we had a Christmas feast of rice and meat curry. We would kill either a pig or a goat for the feast. One year they killed the pig just below my house. In subsequent years (for the sake of my visitors, of course), I asked that the poor animal should be put out of its agony further away; the cries were ear-splitting and heart-rending. Just to humour me, it seemed, the Nepalis did so.

At the feast we sat on the ground in a circle and ate pig curry and rice with our hands from leaf plates. No part of the pig was omitted. All those who were considered to be 'with us' came to the feast. There were usually about 100 people present. There was no celebration of Christmas apart from us, of course. It is, therefore, very thrilling that from 1991, Christmas Day is now a public holiday—a result of the new religious freedom in Nepal.

The service usually included a presentation of the Christmas story by the Sunday-school class. The sheep were the youngest members of the class, dressed up in my white dispensary coats. Their appearance, crawling to Bethlehem, usually brought the house down—as did the ad-libbed conversation of the shepherds before the arrival of the angel. One year the oldest members of the class decided, in addition to the Christmas story, to enact the whole Bible from Genesis to Revelation—a real marathon for all concerned. The performance was quite realistic; towards the end, one of the class was hauled up onto a real cross. The excessive length of the programme presented no problem for the Nepalis. The East is not time-orientated like the West; the present is the important thing. The Nepalis are not always rushing on to something else.

One Christmas, long after my western visitors had given up the futile effort to keep their eyes open, the pastor announced at 10.30 pm that the day was over. He prayed and I took my visitors off to bed. The next day I asked him if they had really finished then. No, he admitted, they had gone on singing, praising and praying until 2 am. The Nepalis would have been up again at five to go out and cut grass for their animals and to carry water. I often felt ashamed of the seeming laziness of my western visitors.

Another Christmas an American couple, Park and Alice Johnson, came to visit. After the Christmas service and feast, Park, Alice and I were sitting upstairs enjoying a quiet cup of tea. Suddenly there was a most tremendous commotion beneath us. We looked out of the window and saw a man, whom I knew well, brandishing his cutting knife and shouting for Hilda and me as he wanted to kill us. Hilda had gone to Pyersingh to keep Pavitri company, so I was the only one available to kill. We watched to see what the Nepalis would do. They handled the situation very well. Half of them engaged the man in conversation and the other half went off to pray. They reasoned with him, and eventually he quietened down and went away with his daughter and son-in-law who, in fact, had been the cause of the trouble. He was angry because they had eaten with us and, therefore, had defiled his Hindu family.

Park and Alice were concerned for my safety, particularly as I had to go up to the dispensary to sleep on the floor. At the time the dispensary was some distance from the other buildings. I was pretty sure that the man would not come again to kill me. He didn't. However, some time later he did have to come to the dispensary, as he was coughing up worms—not a pleasant condition, but not difficult to cure. As the witch doctor had not succeeded in making him better, and we did, he changed his attitude towards us. The irony of the story is that this man died a Christian, but his daughter didn't come near us again.

We were always pleased to welcome the Operation Mobilisation men's teams when they came distributing literature—even when six of them turned up unexpectedly, as they once did in the middle of the rainy season, absolutely starving. They had reckoned on getting food in the villages they visited, but the people didn't have enough for themselves let alone for six hungry visitors. As with the feeding of the five thousand, we seemed to have enough and to spare. We had no shops for emergency supplies, so it was a matter of faith.

These OM team members always made a great contribution to the church. The pastor was very impressed by these talented young men who had given up their time to take the gospel of Jesus Christ to the Nepali villages. One OM-er will always remember his visit to our house. He had carried a generator on their five-day literature trip especially so they could give a slide show to our church group. He was upset to find that the generator would not work. He was in despair. We prayed, but it seemed pretty hopeless. Then someone hit on the idea of stringing together all the torch batteries we had. So we all pooled our torch batteries, and I produced still others that I had in the house. Amazingly, it worked. Those of you who are technically minded might know why the man with the batteries had to lie on the floor and hold them together during the whole performance. He was completely exhausted at the end of it, and the batteries just lasted out. Everyone thought it was a very good show.

I always enjoyed having Ingeborg as a visitor; we had lived together in Tansen. She is a real Norwegian, with plaited fair hair. In the beginning she was in charge of the hospital in the old building in Tansen. Later, when other staff came, she was able to branch out into the work nearest to her heart—maternity. In Tansen she brought many Nepalis into the world and prayed over them at the beginning of their lives. The verse that really summed her up was Philippians 3:13– 'This one thing I do.'

This was true of Ingeborg in all aspects of her life, but particularly in her faith. She would not compromise, feeling rightly that the power of Christ at a delivery case would be hindered if Hindu idols were in the room. If people wanted Ingeborg's help, all their idols had to be removed before she would take the case. She was so highly respected that people gladly did as she requested.

When I moved to Pyersingh, Ingeborg often came to visit us and was a great help. Pavitri went to her for midwifery training. I will always remember one of her visits after Hilda had gone home to England. Ingeborg had a slight fever when she arrived. This increased. As she was the trained health professional, she treated herself, but her temperature kept rising. She stayed in bed while I ran the dispensary. The next day I came up in the middle of the morning to find Ingeborg sitting up outside. Her temperature was 105, she had a headache, and she was not talking sense. I was really worried. It was the middle of the rains, the river was high, and there was no way we could get her to the hospital in Pokhara.

I went back down to the dispensary and got out the medical books. I read everything about fevers, comparing them with her symptoms. In the end, I came to the conclusion that she must have a certain type of malaria. The type I thought she had was likely to develop into cerebral malaria for which, the book said, there was no cure. Ingeborg was allergic to quinine, which was the main anti-malarial drug that we had. What to do? Pray of course—I was already really battering God. Then I remembered that there was a malarial tablet, Daraprim, that Ingeborg might just possibly keep down. Pavitri and I found we had ten tablets between us, and according to the book this was the number of tablets needed for Ingeborg. I gave the tablets to Ingeborg, and to my great relief she didn't vomit them up. Even better, her temperature came down. She continued to improve, but was still very weak.

It was some days before we could move her to Paimey, which was nearer to the road. Then came news that the river was low enough for us to carry her across and take her to Pokhara. Gopal and Churia got one of the Nepali carrying baskets ready for her, and we set off early one morning. The road was still very slippery, so it took us much longer than usual to get to the river. We arrived in time to see a man, who was attempting to cross in front of us, lose his foothold and be swept down the river. We held our breath, and to our relief we saw him crawl out on the other side like a drowned rat. How were we going to get Ingeborg across the river? She couldn't go in the basket, and she was too weak to walk. What to do? The thought of going back up the slippery trail appalled us, but how to get across the river?

We sat down and prayed. As we prayed, out of nowhere, it seemed, appeared a large, strong Nepali man, and he offered us his help. He didn't look like an angel, but he certainly seemed like one to us. With his help, the carriers, Ingeborg and I were able to push upward against the current and get across. We were, of course, soaked to the skin, and Ingeborg was promptly sick. For the rest of the journey to the road, a four-hour walk, Ingeborg kept vomiting over the side of the basket, and saying, 'Let me die here. Please bury me here. Don't trouble about me any more.'

I kept us going by saying, 'Ingeborg, please stay alive until Pokhara where there are Norwegians who can give you a proper burial. I don't think I'd have the strength to bury you here.'

We eventually got to the motor road at 8 pm. There were no buses or any other form of transport on the road. However, while we were wondering what to do, a truck full of goats came along. I asked one of the men sitting in the front if they could take Ingeborg in and give her a seat. The two men sitting next to the driver said they would sit in the back and Ingeborg and I could sit in the front. Churia went in the back and Gopal returned home to take news and supplies.

The goats, after accommodating the three men, were cramped for space, so two of them poked their heads into the front of the truck. Ingeborg was sick out of the window all the way to Pokhara, while the goats huffed and puffed on either side of us. In Pokhara, Churia managed to get a taxi to take us to the leprosarium where Ingeborg's friends were. The wife of the Norwegian was away. I realised how sick Ingeborg was when she said she would sleep with the husband. Happily, that was not necessary.

Ingeborg was taken to the hospital the next day to see the doctor, and in the end she stayed in Pokhara for one month before she was able to return to Tansen. The final straw of this episode for me was that the doctor in Pokhara said that she was vomiting because I had overdosed her with Daraprim—to which my reply was that I thought she was better overdosed than dead. The doctor did admit I had a point.

Besides giving opportunities to prove the power of God, visitors also gave me guidance in decisions I had to make. At one time the UMN asked me to leave Paimey and Pyersingh to go and head up some work they were hoping to start. I did not feel this was God's will for me. To help in the decision, I decided to ask for two signs. One was that my next visitors would say that I was obviously where God wanted me to be.

Shortly after this Dr Tim came to stay for ten days. He was a great help to me in the medical work, and entered into everything we did. He knew nothing about the signs I had asked for regarding my decision.

It was, therefore, a great joy to me when Tim turned to me one day and said, 'This is really the right place for you, Mary, isn't it?'

Since Tim had said this, I felt I should go back to the UMN Health Services Secretary and say I couldn't go where he wanted me to go. As I didn't feel it was scriptural to remain under an authority I couldn't obey, I offered him my resignation from the mission. He accepted it! However, it was necessary to inform the Executive Director of the mission. He 'happened' to come by at that point. When I said I was giving in my resignation, he said, 'You must be joking.' He asked me why I felt that I should not go to this other project. I gave him my reasons. To my great relief, he agreed that I should stay on in Paimey as a member of the UMN, and he would not accept my resignation. And this had been my other sign—that he would see my point of view.

Besides the dispensary work in Paimey, I really enjoyed my Sunday-school class with the young people where I taught reading and Bible classes with all ages. It was a mutual learning situation.

In the early years there were very few schools in Nepal, and only wealthy people could have their children educated outside Nepal. Gradually, however, schools came to all the villages, and as the children became educated they began to read. Because they read out loud, rather than to themselves, this brought new ideas to a wide circle of people. Parents found it hard to face the fact that their sons were not accepting the marriage arrangements they had made, and were thus depriving their parents of a daughter-in-law to help on the farm or with the animals. Boys became ambitious to do other things than just farming or joining the army or getting a poorly-paid job in India. For a long time these had been the only choices open to them. There were, of course, no openings for girls.

One year, one of the items in the school programme was a song written by a twelve-year-old girl who came to the Sunday-school class. She sang about giving girls the opportunity to go to school rather than keeping them as grass-cutters. I never spoke of such things, but by being educated and unmarried, I was showing them there was another way of life than the one they had been brought up to expect as their lot. Several people had said that because I was unmarried I would not fit into a culture where all women are expected to marry. I found the contrary to be the case. The Hindus have their 'bhatinis'—those who were set aside for God—and this they considered I was. I find here in England that pressure is put on people to marry. I was at a conference recently where an internationally-known speaker urged everyone, single or widowed, to picture their ideal man and then prayed for them to meet their 'picture man'. I felt this was sad, since God does definitely speak of the 'gift of a single life'. By urging marriage on all, such speakers could cause some women to miss God's best for their lives.

We were glad when four of our village girls and four village boys won scholarships to the United Mission boarding schools in Kathmandu and Pokhara. Our local village school only went up to Class 7. To go on for higher education, it was necessary to pass the School Leaving Certificate (SLC) exam which is taken in Class 10. Thus our students had to get seats in these boarding schools if they were to have any chance of getting higher education. There were a few local high schools within a day's walk, but their standards were so poor that almost no one who went to them could pass the SLC exams!

Apart from those few who received scholarships to the mission boarding schools, there still remained the problem of how the rest of the students were going to get a chance for advancement. Then one day a boy came into the dispensary for worm medicine. Pavitri knew him and asked what he was doing. He said he was now at a boarding school in Kathmandu. He collected his medicine and went out. Some days later, when I was praying about where the boys should go, I suddenly thought of this boy and his school in Kathmandu. But we knew nothing about it. It was January, and applications for 'town' schools had to be in by December. However, I asked Pavitri the name of the boy and got our boys to speak to him about his school.

They came back with the particulars. It seemed right that they should go to Kathmandu and find out more about the school, although it was a three-day round trip. It was an adventure for them, as none had been to their country's capital before. They stayed with a pastor friend of ours, and came back with details. Yes, they could apply; the entrance exam was in about a month's time.

I knew their families couldn't afford to pay for further education, but I felt I should try to get sponsors for them—although later we were criticised for 'ruining' them with foreign money. I was of two minds whether it was right to take them out of the village. I was swayed in favour of their going by the fact that two out of three lads had to go out of the village anyway to find employment to supplement their family income. Would it not be better for them to be educated and then be able to get better jobs?

Then I had a letter from two Finnish friends saying they wanted to visit us the next Friday and would I let them know if it was all right to come. This was Monday, and unless I sent a personal messenger to Kathmandu there would have been no way I could let them know. I suddenly realised that if the three boys were to go for their entrance exams for the school they would have to go on Wednesday. They could take the message to our Finnish friends that it was all right to come. So off they went on Wednesday with the letter to our visitors.

On Friday evening I looked across the valley to the trail on which they would all be coming. I was anxious to hear what news they would bring. I was still in two minds—was I doing the right thing? I was wondering, for example, how I was ever going to pay for their schooling. Then I saw the three boys and our two visitors. I went out to meet them. What had happened? They were jubilant. They had all passed and been accepted at the school.

The story they then told was amazing to me. After they had sat and passed the entrance exam, the headmaster, very rightly, wanted to know how they were going to get their fees paid. I had sent letters with them, but he, of course, didn't know me. He asked them if they knew anyone in Kathmandu. They mentioned the Finnish lady to whom they had to take my letter. The headmaster was delighted, as she was the only westerner he knew in Kathmandu and furthermore, she was already paying for two orphan boys in the school. She came, paid the deposit for our boys, and said she would pay their fees at the same time as she paid the orphans' fees.

She told us she had been praying for Christian

boys to go to the school to keep her boys company. She asked how I had known there were vacancies in the school. They had only just been advertised in a Kathmandu paper, and she wondered if I had seen it. I had not, of course. We all gave thanks together. I shall never forget two of the boys' prayers. One said to God that we were sorry we had made him 'wakko biyo' (sick to the back teeth) with our prayers when he had the answer all the time. The other said, 'God, it seemed so complicated when we were trying to do it ourselves, but when you took over it all went so smoothly.'

Once again, I was thankful to visitors for confirming to me that I had heard God correctly. Within a couple of years, nineteen young people were going to that school in Kathmandu.

Another visitor was able to open doors of help for me, which would not have happened if she had not come. I was in Pokhara and unexpectedly met one of our Interserve missionaries, Jane Dingle, who was on holiday from India. The people with whom she was staying had to go away. They said she could stay in their house, but I suggested she came back with me, which she was happy to do.

I had been away for a few days, but news of my return had worked through the bush telegraph system, and next morning people started arriving and arriving. For some reason I cannot remember, my Nepali helpers were away and I was on my own, registering, diagnosing, treating, and giving injections. Thankfully, Jane was a nurse, so she was able to help. We had about 175 patients, a lot of whom were very sick with difficult problems. When we had seen about 100, we decided to ask the local patients with less serious illnesses to come the next day.

I was used to the pressure, but Jane was horrified and, I thought, over-reacted to my situation. She said, 'Interserve says they are a caring mission; where's their care for you when they leave you in a situation like this on your own?' I tried to explain that in Nepal, Interserve was a member of the United Mission and it was UMN who made decisions about personnel. UMN had to cover their own projects and had no one to spare to help me. I was just being pig-headed in staying here anyway!

Jane insisted on writing to the mission, telling them of the immense pressures I was under and that it was up to them to do something for me. I was very grateful to her for caring, but as I knew there were certain mission policies involved in all this, I did not hold out much hope of help. However, I was wrong. The person in charge of Interserve at that point was a good friend of mine, but for various reasons he felt his hands were tied. However, with Jane's letter in his hand, he went to the Health Services Secretary. She was Norwegian, new to the position, and so to find out more about me she spoke to her good friend and mine, Ingeborg.

Most of us are more dependent than we realise on what our friends say about us. The next thing I knew was that, first Marlene, and then Hanne, both nurses, were seconded to me for a few months each. I think they would say it was a good experience for them. Val Collett, who eventually came to help me, was sent to explore community health possibilities in the area. Then Helen Matthews, a nurse working in Tansen, felt God was calling her to come and start community health work in the area. So, to my great joy, Helen was with me for over a year and covered my leave at home. A Dutch nurse, Sjordje, was seconded to be with her.

When I got back from leave, a new Health Services Secretary had been appointed. Helen was to go to a different UMN project, and again there was no one available to help me. I went back to Paimey on my own, to consider, I was told, closing down the work there as soon as possible.

It had always been my prayer and longing that the district should not be without medical help when I left. Over the years we had hoped that several Nepalis who had gone for training would feel called to take over, but for one reason and another, they didn't. The dispensary work was heavy, and I only had Pavitri part-time to help me. Patients were coming to the dispensary from over a day's walk away. It didn't seem right to close when there was no other help in the area. But what to do? I also wanted to have time to go on teaching and helping the church. I was in despair. I remember getting down on my knees and praying, 'God, have you no one in the world who could come to help me?'

It was a rather dreary Saturday afternoon and I heard a call outside. I went out to find one of the boys who was at the boarding school in Pokhara standing on the veranda with a visitor. I do not know if Elaine had ever been the answer to anyone's prayer before, but she was to mine.

Elaine had come on a visit to Kashmir. On the way she decided to visit two doctor friends in Pokhara. When she got there, she realised that it was not a good time to travel as it was the beginning of the rainy season. By order of the Nepalese government, the

Pokhara Boarding School had just changed from Nepali to English medium for teaching. They were, in consequence, needing help to get their pupils up to the required standard in English. Elaine decided that she would delay her visit to Kashmir and stay in Pokhara and respond to this need. When the end of the school term came, her friends, the two doctors, suggested she come to visit me. They had been my visitors a few months earlier.

So Elaine arrived to spend part of the school holiday with me. Now Elaine was not a teacher, but a nurse. When she saw my need, she realised that it was even greater than that at the boarding school. The headmaster also agreed with us. So for several months Elaine came to help me.

When it was nearly time for Elaine to leave, I had another visitor. Jean had been in Kathmandu with Youth With A Mission and Operation Mobilisation, and had been helping out in the Social Work Department in Patan Hospital. While there, she heard about me and decided to come out for a few days' holiday. (I remember she hoped to get some of her knitting done!) The person she was relieving in Kathmandu was returning, and Jean didn't know what she should do for the next few months before she returned to England. Now Jean was not a social worker, but a nurse. So Jean came after Elaine.

Aino was from Finland. While she was in language school in Kathmandu, her mother died and she had to go back to Finland. When she came back, the UMN decided that it would be good for her to be somewhere where she heard mostly Nepali. So I was asked if Aino could come to me for a few months. Aino was a nurse. So she came after Jean.

Ginger was an Interserve missionary in India. Her visa was not renewed for India. It was decided to send Ginger to work in Nepal. She was to come to the United Mission to Nepal's language school. What to do with Ginger for the few months before the language school started? Send her to Mary! Ginger was a nurse. So after Aino came Ginger.

Val Collett had felt for some time she would like to come and carry on the area community health programme which had been started by Helen. We had done what we could, but with no one else working full-time in that area it was difficult to achieve much. Val is an Interserve missionary, and to my great joy it was agreed that she should come to help me with the community health programme and the handing over of the medical work to Nepalis. I had always said that without help I couldn't keep the day-to-day work going and, at the same time, do all the clearing up and handing over that was involved. So after Ginger, came Val—and Val was a nurse. Due to another change in the Health Services Secretary, Kate Skinner, also a nurse, was allowed to come to help us.

The plan that God had for us for the future was not clear. The church was in the hands of the Nepali pastor, but who would be willing to come to such an isolated place, with little or no encouragement, to run the dispensary? It could only be someone whom God had called. But where was he or she?

I had an appointment to go to Kathmandu to discuss the situation with the new UMN Health Services Secretary. I set off at dawn down the trail to get the early bus into Kathmandu so that I would arrive in time to keep my appointment. I got on the first bus that came along, but it was very slow. I thought we would never get there. Ordinary Nepali buses are not really comfortable. There was also the hazard that people, not used to travelling on buses, would very often be sick just where they were and, you hoped, not just where you were. It is not a good thing to open the bus window, especially if there is a wind blowing and the person in front of you decides to be sick out of his window. Many times I have had to close my window to avoid the spray. It is also not unknown for the bus to break down—which is what it did on this occasion.

I climbed out and sat on the side of the road, feeling very cross with God that he had not arranged a better bus. I told him there was no hope now of reaching Kathmandu in time for my appointment, and no possibility of getting another one. Some people might be horrified that I should speak with God like that, but besides being my God whom I worship and adore, he had been my only companion for much of my time in Nepal—and sometimes you just talk to your friends that way.

As I sat on the road complaining to God, along came a comfortable-looking landrover with an Englishman sitting in the front. Before I had time to signal them, they had sailed past. I started complaining to God again, 'You might have made them stop; can't you do better than this?' Then to my utter amazement, I looked up and saw the landrover backing down the road towards me. A Nepali man in the back leaned out and asked if I was hoping to get to Kathmandu. I explained that I was, but as he could see, the bus had broken down. He offered me a lift, and with great joy I climbed in and had one of the most comfortable and quickest trips to Kathmandu I had ever had. I had to apologise to God.

I got to Kathmandu on time for my appointment with the Health Services Secretary. After talking for some time, he casually mentioned two trained Nepalis, husband and wife, who had asked about coming to work in Paimey. I knew them both. He didn't know where they were now and whether they had left Kathmandu or not. I didn't know where to find them.

There was a wedding on Sunday and, unexpectedly, I got an invitation. Imagine my surprise when half way through the wedding, this couple walked in! I was able to talk to them afterwards, and they confirmed that they felt God was calling them to work in Paimey. On the way home from the wedding I felt as if my heart would burst with joy. It was not just an ordinary feeling but a supernatural one. I just knew they were the ones God had chosen to take over from me.

There were many trials and difficulties in the months that followed, and sometimes it seemed as if they would never come. But that experience God had given me helped me when it seemed almost impossible that they would ever arrive. But, praise the Lord, they did. It was an added joy that they are the children of the two couples who first came into Nepal with Hilda. They had played together in Nautanwa when Hilda Steele and Pat O'Hanlon were there, before the land of Nepal had opened. They had come into Nepal with their parents and later married each other. So the work had come full circle.

19

Conflicting Ideals

Missionaries and mission tend to have a bad press. Most people think it's a good thing to help the poor, but would prefer that you don't mix religion with it. Even in the churches, the missionary meeting and prayer meeting get the poorest attendance or are non-existent. If you don't mention the words 'mission' or 'missionary' and bill the meeting as an adventurous exploration of the 'back of beyond', people will pay to come to it. Because of the 'spiritual' and 'secular' sides of missions, working as a missionary provides more areas for conflict than working with an aid programme does.

When I was at a language assessment course before I went to Nepal, I remember fierce arguments between those who felt that Christians should live 'by faith' and accept what God sent and not look for any regular salary, and those who said that 'a workman was worthy of his hire' and therefore deserved at least a cost-of-living allowance. On the question of giving, one group felt that people should be told of needs and so be informed in their giving; the other group felt that entire reliance should be placed on God to stir the hearts of his people to give.

Some mission agencies do pay much more than others. In the United Mission to Nepal we were all on different allowances, according to the policy of our sending missions. Interestingly, it was not the 'poor' among us that were so concerned but rather the 'rich' when they discovered how little their colleagues were receiving. Pay was not something we discussed. The 'rich' had asked the UMN treasurer for the different rates of pay received by each mission. When they knew, they requested from their own sending missions a reduction in their allowances. All of us were paid a flat rate, regardless of the number of years we had been in the mission or our qualifications. Thus, the senior surgeon who had been around for thirty years would be getting the same allowance as the newest recruit who might have no paper qualification. This never created problems.

However, the type of work, the hours worked, and the pressure of the job do bring problems. A woman doctor, whose husband was assigned to a remote area, experienced a lot of stress. There was no medical work in the area. The local people, discovering she was a doctor, besieged her house morning, noon and night. This put great strain on her and her family. Trained as she was to relieve suffering, she found it hard to refuse people treatment. However, she had a duty to her husband and family. When she became pregnant the stress mounted, until her husband told the local officials that, as she was expecting a baby, she couldn't see patients. This was accepted, possibly because the officials were men and not so affected as the women were; the men, being more mobile, could get treatment elsewhere. The need to withhold her services, however, continued to be a great source of heartache and conflict for the wife. The stress was later relieved when the mission set up a small dispensary in the area.

Even missions and missionaries can be 'success'-orientated, but spiritual results cannot be assessed as easily as physical results. As I write this there is a programme on the radio about the salaries of English clergy and how they should be determined; one suggestion was by the number of people they got to heaven! A friend of mine spoke of working in one country and seeing no 'spiritual' results. He was then transferred to another country and there was an immediate response. He said, 'What had changed?' After only a short plane trip he certainly hadn't changed, neither had his methods. Maybe in the second place there had been a lot of prayer and people had laboured sacrificially, as it were, 'laying down their lives for the gospel', but they had seen no fruit. So my friend arrived to hearts already prepared by the Holy Spirit.

In one new area where missionaries went to work in Nepal, three were invalided home with nervous breakdowns, one lost her visa, another narrowly escaped death falling off a roof, and yet another was invalided home for physical illness. Until the inimical forces in that area were bound in the name of Jesus, these casualties continued. When we go as servants of Jesus Christ, we are waging war against the forces of evil, a fact which many westerners choose to disbelieve or ignore. Also, the Bible records that there were places where Christ could do no great work because of people's unbelief.

God has given us equipment for this warfare, but because we do not recognise the battle we're in, we often don't use God's weapons. I am amazed that even after fifty years as a Christian, I can find myself with my 'shield of faith' down and my 'breastplate of right-eousness' off. Our subtle foe has been up to his tricks longer than any of us have been around. But then, so has God! God has given us weapons and put them into our hands for us to use. We have to take them and make our stand.

In one translation of Ephesians 6:13, it says, 'Having done all, stand.' In a certain situation I was facing, I said to a friend, 'I have done all. You name it, I've done it. Praising, praying, resisting, binding, loosing, seeking others' advice, confronting, working, repenting.' She said, 'Well, now you just have to stand.' I am still 'standing' in that situation. I remember gaining comfort, when I was feeling particularly unfruitful, from a friend's prayer: 'Lord, you have not called us to be successful, but faithful.'

'Appropriate technology' is part of mission jargon these days. This means taking help that is appropriate to the needs of the people in the area where you serve. You don't go with a previously thought-out package and just offload it onto the local people. You go and discuss with them, and then bring what the people themselves feel they most need. One friend who did this was surprised to find it was not water, education, electricity or medical help that the people most wanted and—none of which they had. They asked first of all for assistance to stop their land from being washed away. Because of deforestation and monsoon rains, they were losing more and more of the land on which they grew their crops. If this went on, they would cease to exist as a community, which would render all other benefits useless. My friend was able to give this help.

The most blatant example of inappropriate technology I saw in Nepal was the giving of an X-ray plant to a hospital. The need was there, and the hospital stated what they required. The donors, however, had their own ideas. They were very generous and so gave the biggest and best. Very commendable, but sadly they failed to realise there was not the electricity available to run it. So it became the hospital's most prized white elephant.

When we went into Nepal there were those who would not join the United Mission because we were not free to evangelise but were only permitted to 'practise our own religion'. Those who joined represented a broad spectrum of Christian belief. There were many who gloomily predicted that theologically we would blow ourselves to pieces. How could those who were labelled 'liberals' possibly work with those who were 'evangelicals'? We need to look beneath our labels; they may or may not have much to do with our Christian practice. It was the 'liberals' who had daily prayers for the staff each day at 7 am in the hospital chapel and were themselves present. They could also be found on their knees with an open Bible in the early hours. Whereas it was an 'evangelical' who changed the chapel to a physiotherapy room, causing the services to cease. We all, it seems, get caught out on the 'judging business'. Miraculously, the UMN survived and was forty years old in 1994.

It was gloriously liberating to go with fresh good news to people who had never heard that Jesus Christ is good news. Jesus is a life-enhancer, not a life-limiter. He said, 'I am come that you might have life and have it more abundantly.' It is to give us freedom that Christ came: 'If Jesus makes you free, you will indeed be free.' In Nepal we saw people coming to realise the freedom they would have in Christ, not only release from costly Hindu ceremonies, but also from things in their personalities and culture to which they were in bondage. When I asked Nepali wives about the freedoms they had found since they became Christians, I was surprised how often they replied, 'Oh, my husband doesn't get drunk and beat me any more.'

Healing from diseases for which the witch doctor had no cure was another area which caused people to think about the freedom they could have in Christ. Two groups of people, TB and leprosy patients, had to spend long periods in hospital. They had time and opportunity to hear the Christian message and observe the lives of those proclaiming it. God worked in the hearts of many of these patients. They returned to their distant villages cured or with the disease arrested. They started to experience the power of praying to Jesus, and of seeing children, relatives or neighbours cured. They threw away family religious objects. When they took this risky step, others watched closely to see if disaster would strike. When it didn't, whole families and villages became Christian.

There has been amazing church growth in Nepal, but this brings its own problems. A letter this week from a friend who was in prison for his faith says, 'For the first time in my career in Nepal I was ready to pack it in and tell Nepal goodbye. What police, prison and politics couldn't do, God's people were just about successful in doing. Only the knowledge that this is where God wants me kept me going.' I know the feeling. He tells how a close friend and a church leader nearly split the church over a small matter. A leader refused to consider reconciliation with his pastor.

Some Christians cheated and were deceitful in land purchases. Sadly, there is nothing new.

The position of women in the church came up when we were in Nepal. The men missionaries didn't want to take the communion services, so they asked two women to do so, which they did. It didn't seem to create a problem for anyone and when a Nepali pastor was appointed, he naturally took over. There was one missionary, however, who objected to women leading in the church. The pastor was in charge, but at that time all his helpers, apart from this missionary, were women. The missionary believed that 'leadership is male'. To my surprise, all the Nepali women handed in their resignations and told the men to get on with it. It lasted for a few weeks. I felt very concerned. A wise woman named Betty, who had been a missionary in China, said, 'Don't worry, Mary, this sort of thing always happens. We had a church in China nearly split over women wearing hats.' We owed a lot to this woman. She was always going up the mountain behind the hospital to pray for us. She had a happy knack of being able to defuse situations. She was also the most coveted speaker at our Sunday evening get-togethers.

A business manager decided to put up a chart giving our positions in the team in order of seniority. He was paving the way for CVs, job descriptions and management structures. Up to then we had all accepted each other, helped out where necessary, and done any job that needed to be done. Missionaries should be above such petty squabbles. However, feelings ran high. Betty looked at the list and in a 'throw-off' sort of manner said, 'Well, I'm below the bottom line.' She helped to fold the laundry. Suddenly we all saw how stupid we were being, and laughed.

It is part of Nepali culture not to say thank you. We used to find it strange to give someone a present and not to be thanked for it. They thought we were obsessed with saying thank you. Later, when I asked my Nepali friends about this, they explained that of course they were grateful for any present you gave them. Anyone would know that, you didn't have to be told so. I'm not sure how much not saying thank you stems from the Hindu concept of obtaining merit with the gods for your actions. If you are thanked, you have already received your reward on earth.

We always charged a small sum for medicine. We learned over the years that free medicine was not appreciated. In fact, I was told I should charge more for the injections, as then they would be considered more beneficial. Of course, if people really couldn't pay, we gave charity. High-caste Brahmins, who were usually not poor, were the most reluctant to pay. Some even said I would lose merit if I charged them, the theory being that to serve a Brahmin was to gain merit. People assumed that was surely why I was serving in that remote area. No one with any sense would do it for any other reason–unless, of course, my government was paying me a large salary! Anyway, in their view I was definitely on my way to make myself richer one way or the other. One got used to not being thanked, though it was very nice when one was.

Our regard for time was another way in which we differed from the Nepalis. I used to have a Bible class each week with the pastor. He was supposed to come at 7.30 am. Sometimes he came at 6.15 am, at other times 9.30 am, and on occasions he didn't turn up at all. He never saw any necessity to apologise for his change of time or non-appearance. He assumed I would of course know that if he could come he would, and that if he couldn't, then I would understand that a situation had arisen that must take precedence over a prior arrangement. Now that Nepalis are moving into a democratic way of life, perhaps they will become more time-orientated. Certainly, a flexible attitude to time can be very unstressful—provided one is prepared for it.

To me it was interesting that the true hill farmer came mostly for worms, diarrhoea, sores, fevers and accidents: diseases associated with lack of hygiene, simple lifestyle (having to hull their rice, cut their grass, pound their grain by hand), from parasites or the mountainous terrain in which they lived. When the schoolmasters or more educated people came, it was a different story. We had then to think about stress-related diseases, such as gastric ulcers.

I began to puzzle about this. In some cases it was because they had read about these diseases and so began to worry that they might have them. But it was not just autosuggestion; some really did develop the complaint. In the beginning we never saw a case of appendicitis unless the person had association with western culture. This has now changed, perhaps because of the arrival of white bread and other changes in dietary habits. One would think it much more stressful for a hill farmer, who had nothing if his crops failed, as they frequently did, than for a schoolmaster who, in theory at least, had a regular salary coming in. This, however, did not seem to be the case.

The mountains of Nepal act like a magnet to some people. One person who came to work with me asked if I felt the call of the mountains was enough. I gave an unequivocal, 'No.'

Brian, an expatriate, came to Nepal with a definite call from God, but he also had in his blood the call of the mountains. He used to sit in his headmaster's office and feel them drawing him like a magnet. It is interesting that his mother, when she was carrying him, couldn't stop reading books about mountains. This was not so with any of her other children.

Brian and his family were great walkers. Brian himself did several climbs, but his great ambition in life was to reach Mardi Peak in the Annapurna range. He talked with a fellow missionary climber, Gunnar, a Dane, and they decided to make an attempt at it. As they were both experienced climbers, they decided they would go on their own. They set off and after a long ascent to the base of the mountains, they pitched their tent and made for the summit, which they reached mid-afternoon on Tuesday. They roped themselves together and started back down the mountain. Then, in a difficult place, Gunnar stumbled, and in so doing jerked the rope, causing Brian to fall. When Gunnar got up to Brian he found him coughing up blood. Brian was not able to walk on at that point. Gunnar helped him into a crevice in the mountainside. As it was very cold, Gunnar decided to go and collect their sleeping bags from their tent, which they had pitched lower down.

As Gunnar set off to collect the sleeping bags, dusk was falling. After he had started he realised he didn't know where to go. So after searching around for a while he decided to retrace his steps to Brian. Then came the terrible realisation that he had lost his way back. He wandered around desperately in search of

Brian. Night came. Gunnar realised that unless he kept awake, moving and walking, he would die of exposure. So he walked about all that night and the next day. He eventually found the tent and crawled inside and slept. When he awoke, he again searched and searched for Brian, but couldn't find him. By now it was Thursday. Then Friday came, then Saturday. As Gunnar wandered about he suddenly saw a small hut with a woman in the doorway. He tried to speak to her but she wouldn't answer. He thought he could stay with her. She went inside the igloo-like hut and came out with an idol in her hand. This puzzled Gunnar and he didn't know what to do next. While he was wondering, she disappeared. Then to his great delight he saw Brian coming towards him across the snow. As fast as he could, he went to him. He called out, 'Brian, Brian,' but Brian took no notice, and walked on past him and disappeared.

Puzzled and disillusioned, Gunnar tried to find the path back so he could get help. Then he spotted a coach with a great party of people. Speaking of it afterwards, Gunnar said he did wonder how they had got there. He was, however, so delighted to see them that he rushed towards them as fast as he could, only to find that when he got close, they too disappeared.

In the meantime their wives, Beulah and Eva, were beginning to worry. I arrived to stay with Beulah on Thursday, the day Brian and Gunnar had been expected back. I met Beulah in Pokhara bazaar, and she said, 'Brian was due back from his mountain trip, but he hasn't come yet. However, there is still time. He said if there was a mist or something they would wait to make a final attempt. They said they would definitely be back tomorrow, as Brian is taking part in the Nepali Christian Fellowship conference.'

So that night we didn't worry, thinking they would turn up next day. Eva, who had one son aged two, was expecting again; but she also had hepatitis, so couldn't go out. She was being looked after in the mission compound.

When Brian and Gunnar had not arrived back by Friday evening, we were really anxious. On Saturday morning Beulah and I met with other people in the mission to discuss sending a search party. Two mission personnel, who had experience in climbing, said they would go. Also an experienced Nepali, who climbed regularly in the area, happened to be in Pokhara. He delayed his return to Kathmandu to go with them. We had to collect together equipment and food. It was Sunday morning before the party was able to set off.

The next evening I had to go to the Nepal Christian Fellowship. When I got back Beulah came to meet me, and as soon as I saw her I knew Brian was dead. But the amazing thing was that Gunnar was alive and well. The search party had met him on Monday afternoon. They had seen him from a distance, trudging down the main trail. When they met him he just couldn't believe they were real, and when he did, he couldn't stop talking. They had discussed going on to look for Brian, but realised it was too difficult and too dangerous. Furthermore, there was no way he could be alive after nearly a week in the condition in which Gunnar had left him.

So they turned around and walked back with Gunnar. He went on to his wife and son, while the rest of the party came to tell Beulah and her three daughters.

It was strange. We had lived in a sort of enclosed world of hope. We had lived together through many emotions, day and night. Beulah had already made up her mind that she would go home with her daughters should Brian be dead. This was a good thing, since suddenly it felt that the whole world was descending on them with their views and opinions.

Beulah was wonderful. The next day she went and spoke of her husband's death at the Nepali Christian Fellowship conference. She spoke of the certainty of life after death and how she knew that she would meet her husband again. It was a powerful testimony, and all could see how wonderfully God was sustaining her now in her time of need. For years afterwards Nepalis who were at the conference would speak of it.

Gunnar came with the director of the mission and told Beulah and me all that had happened. I was amazed he could do it. He only faltered once, when telling how he had left Brian in the cave. He broke down and said, 'He was my friend, my friend.'

Brian seemed to have had a premonition that he was to die soon. Before he went, Beulah had laughed about them celebrating their twenty-fifth wedding anniversary, and Brian had said, 'Oh, I won't be here for that.' He spent his last night at home writing to a close friend, warning him to repent and accept Christ as his Saviour before it was too late. The man got the letter after Brian was dead. These and other small incidents just before his death convinced Beulah that Brian had sensed he was going to die. Beulah, of course, had her own regrets over what she had and had not said on the night before Brian went on the trek. He had promised it would be his last one.

Eva told of Gunnar's return. She had someone helping her with her little boy. The person was out of the room when Eva saw the door opening. She didn't look up at first, but when she did she saw Gunnar standing there. She went wild with excitement. 'What did Gunnar say?' I asked.

'He thought I was over-emotional,' she replied.

Later in the night, she kept feeling him to make certain he was still beside her.

A search party went up later to look for Brian's body, but never found it. Beulah did take her daughters home to New Zealand, where they are all doing well. Gunnar and Eva continued with the mission for several more years.

For me, Mardi Peak will always remind me of Brian. He was a lovely man. I have often imagined that when Brian arrived in heaven God said to him, 'Well Brian, I let you die where you most wanted to be—in the mountains.'

20

All for All

If I find him, if I follow,
Is he sure to bless?
Saints, apostles, prophets, martyrs,
Answer, 'Yes.'

It is, however, all for all. The Nepali Christians know this; they had to face leaving all they had. But, like the man in Matthew 13:46, in finding Jesus they found the pearl of great price and so were prepared to give up all to follow him. Jesus himself said, 'Whosoever he be of you that forsaketh not all that he has, he cannot be my disciple.'

Churia forsook all that he had. He had five children and a smallholding of land when his father disinherited him and turned him out of his home. He moved into their buffalo shed with the children. He went out early each morning and came back late at night, for the local authorities were looking for him to put him in prison. One evening, after his wife had cooked all the food they had for their evening supper, Churia's father came and threw mud into it. To the parents' amazement, the older children turned to their grandfather and said, 'Be careful, grandfather, what you are doing; we are children of the Living God, and he will take care of us.' The parents feared this would bring the wrath of the grandfather down on them even more, but the opposite was the case. Though he did disinherit his son, he never troubled them again. God did look after that family. One son is now a health worker, another is in the Indian Army, another is working in Kathmandu, and two others are being educated in Kathmandu.

I myself have seen him give me back a hundred-fold more than I ever gave up for him. I left a flat in Reading and have come back to a cottage in the garden of England left to me by a friend while I was in Nepal. It is a hundred times more a 'desirable residence' than the one I gave up to go to Nepal in 1957.

When I went to Nepal, my allowance was £25 a month, and the last allowance I received in Nepal, thirty-three years later, was £83 a month. But I have lacked for nothing. This allowance was only possible because of the sacrificial gifts of my friends and home church. I have travelled more than many of my friends who stayed in their career paths at home. I have gained many friends in Nepal and in other countries in the world who have come to mean as much to me as any relatives; truly, this is the hundredfold that Jesus promised.

It has been a privilege to be in circumstances where again and again I have seen God proved to be a promise-keeping God. He has supplied my needs and the needs of those around me so many times. One story that I love to tell happened in 1960. I received a letter from Pokhara saying that the Queen of England was coming and would I come and be presented to her. She was to arrive in about two weeks. The problem was, what to wear! There was no time to get any special clothes. I had a fairly respectable suit (bought for £5) and a white, chunky sort of hat. So far so good, but I had to have a pair of white gloves. This was a must in those days, if one was presented to the Queen. What to do? All enquiries drew a blank. I prayed and wondered.

A friend in England was in the habit of sending food parcels and one arrived just then. I opened it and took out the usual, most welcome, food. Then I came across a small parcel, and with it a letter from my friend. 'I know you will think I am mad to send these, but Janet your goddaughter (then aged eight) insisted that I send them to you. She took her own pocket money and went to Woolworths to buy them. We have all said you won't have any use for them in the mountain jungle where you live, but Janet said you must have them. So I have put them in!'

When I opened the parcel, there was a pair of white gloves! If I had taken my hat round the shops and tried to match gloves with it, I couldn't have done better. They were also my size; I have large hands and often have difficulty getting gloves large enough to fit me. The timing, too, was so wonderful. The parcel had been sent off from England at least six months earlier, and yet it arrived in the fortnight before I was to be presented. It could so easily have arrived too late, or too early, but God was in charge of the timing.

There was no motor road in those days between Pokhara and Tansen (where I worked at the time); we had to walk three days in order to be presented. Dr O'Hanlon told the Queen that we had walked over the hills to come to see her, and she turned to Prince Philip and remarked on this. She did not, however, hear the minor miracle of my white gloves which made it possible for me to meet her at all.

A very different need was met one year in the

middle of the rainy season. I received a letter from my solicitor telling me about the house my friend had left me. He sent certain legal documents for me to sign as soon as possible, as my friend was dying of terminal cancer and wanted to bequeath the house to me before she died. The problem was that I had to get a notary public or similar legal official to witness my signature. The puzzle was where to find such a person in the rainy season in the middle of Nepal? I asked the local headman if he could help or give any advice, but he could not. I might find such a person if I went to Kathmandu but that would involve a journey of about twelve days there and back; there were no roads and the planes from Pokhara often didn't fly in the rains. What should I do? Pray, of course, but what else?

Soon after, I was finishing the evening chores and cleaning the oil lamps when I heard a shout from the back of the house. Down the slippery path came an American. We were surprised to see him, as we tended to be cut off from outside visitors during the rains. He turned out to be an American Peace Corps volunteer who was stationed at the area office in our district. He had been near us doing some work for the Nepali government, heard we were in the area, and decided to come and spend the night with us. He was the nearest thing to a notary public that it would have been possible to find in Nepal at that time. He gladly agreed to witness my signature and took the papers to the local office to put the official stamp on them. They passed as legal in England, and I received the house.

As I have said, Paimey and Pyersingh were about a forty-eight mile walk from Tansen, where we obtained our medical supplies for the dispensary, our post and most of our food. It took the carriers five or six days for the round trip. Our diet was mainly rice, lentils, local grain and vegetables, with meat very occasionally when an animal was killed. As my friends will testify, I am very fond of potatoes. There were none to be found locally and they proved difficult to grow. It is impossible to describe the yearning one gets for certain foodstuffs when far from home. I used to say I had more sympathy for Esau, who sold his birthright for a pot of lentils, than I had before I went to Nepal. Not that I would have sold mine for a pot of lentils, but on occasions I would have done so for a bar of chocolate or some Marmite. On this occasion, it was potatoes for which I yearned. I knew there were supposed to be some on the next load. We always looked forward to the arrival of the men back from Tansen, bringing with them our two or three weeks' mail, the much-needed medical supplies and our 'luxury' food.

After the usual enquiries about our friends in Tansen, how the journey had gone and so forth, and having given the men some much-needed refreshment, we got down to opening the load. I usually unpacked the food. I quickly looked for the potatoes but couldn't find any. I asked the men and they said they had not brought them. They had their priorities; rice we needed, potatoes we could live without.

Hilda was sympathetic, but not being so dependent on food for her happiness, she couldn't understand why I was so upset. I was feeling really grumpy. Hilda went on sorting out our mail. She called out, 'Here's a parcel for you from Germany.' What a pleasant surprise. It was a large bulky packet, whatever could it be? I wasn't expecting anything. Imagine my surprise when I opened it and found dehydrated potato, enough to supply us with potato until the men went on their next trip in three weeks' time. Another time I had a great longing for a packet of tomato soup, and one arrived in the next post from a friend in England. It was always exciting to get a parcel; in fact, the arrival of mail from home was one of the highlights of our lives, not having many other built-in diversions. Can God spread a table in the wilderness? Yes, he can and does.

I'm glad that I have had the privilege of living among the Nepalis. Their courage and resourcefulness are known across the world through those who joined the Gurkha regiments. I have seen these qualities again and again among the hill people of Nepal. While I would be looking for a piece of string, they would be making some out of a stalk. The people in the area where I lived grew maize corn and survived on it for half the year, and for the other half had millet. None of the corn was wasted. The kernels are eaten or ground to make bread or porridge; the inside of the cob is burnt on the fire; the husks and leaves are used to make mats, and the stalks are used for making fences. No throwaway paper plates for them or piles of washing up. Feast-day plates were made from leaves, neatly sewn together with bits of stalk.

It was lovely to live among people who came to faith in Jesus uncluttered by the materialism, unbelief and theological uncertainties of the West. A clergyman who wrote a book called *Your God is Still Too Small* asked me if Jyoti's goats really were dead (Chapter 16). He went on cross-questioning me and was finding it difficult to believe they really came alive. I thought if Jyoti could hear and understand our conversation she would marvel at the smallness of his God still. He has since written, and said that he now believes God can raise goats from the dead!

Having seen how gladly Nepalis accept Jesus and rejoice at being free from bondage to Hindu gods, I find it distressing to see people in the West going after Transcendental Meditation and New Age philosophies, most of which are based on Eastern religions, especially Hinduism.

I was walking in Kathmandu one day with two of our children from Paimey. We met an English woman who was wondering about becoming a Hindu or a Buddhist. After she had gone, I explained to the children what she had been saying. One of them looked up at me with big eyes and said, 'Aunty, she can't know our Jesus can she?' I thought, how true; that child had got more of the crux of the matter than many of us in the West. Those who really know Jesus and accept him as Lord would never see anything in other religions. Just before I came home to England to retire, one of my Nepali friends who was having to report to the police each month said to me, 'Mary, do not worry. We will not go back whatever they do to us. What else is there worth living for except Jesus?'

I often think how much I would have missed had I not been obedient to God's call to go to Nepal. I would have missed the opportunity to be utterly dependent on God, which is not so possible here at home. I would have missed the privilege of experiencing him as my only resource and finding him utterly reliable. I would have missed the joy of sharing in the beauty of Nepal and its rugged hills, and sharing in the wisdom and courage of its country people.

As I write, there is a talk on the television on organic farming. Our Nepali mail-runner decided, after a few years of taking the free handouts of fertiliser, that he didn't want any more. He went back to putting the buffalo and goat manure on his land, as that gave him much better crops. Yesterday there was a talk on the radio in which it was said that in the West we have let one half of our brain die and rely only on the reasoning side. I am glad that I have spent thirty-three years of my life with people who have both sides of their brain working all the time; long may it continue to do so!

Major changes have taken place in Nepal and there is new freedom. One hopes and prays—and I invite you to join me in praying—that the new freedom may be based on the only true freedom, that which is given by God, who made us all and sent his Son into the world that all might believe in him and have everlasting life. He that has the Son, Jesus, has life. Jesus said, 'I am come that you might have life and have it more abundantly.' If Jesus makes you free, you will be free indeed.

The church in Nepal needs prayer for wisdom to handle its new freedom. So far it has been remarkably united, probably because of the opposition it has endured, but it is facing problems it has not had before. It is exciting to hear of many becoming Christians, and wonderful to know of many Nepalis with real zeal to evangelise their country. Sadly, however, there are cults and heresies coming in with confusing doctrines for young believers.

The country is still a Hindu kingdom. The statute books still say that it is against the law for a Nepali to change from the religion of his fathers, and he can be punished for so doing. However, alongside this, Muslim, Christian and Buddhist special celebration days are now government-sanctioned holidays. It is possible to write freely about and advertise other religions than Hinduism. Christian books can now be printed in the country. The church can receive financial aid from overseas. Church buildings and land can be registered. How to administer this aid, so that the money may be used to build up and not weaken the church, is a matter for much prayer.

I hope this book will inspire and help many to love and serve the Nepali people. I hope, too, that it will help any who might be wondering if the cost of following Jesus might be too great. The cost of not following is much greater.

Postscript

On a recent trip to Nepal I found tremendous changes in many areas but the village people were to a large extent still influenced by their traditional customs. Here are a few examples.

Pollution

To be greeted in Kathmandu by cyclists with their noses and mouths covered with face masks was a sad experience. This is a common practice because of the air pollution in the city.

Politics

The King has relinquished absolute power, and Nepal now has a democratic government. Currently the Congress party is in power, with the main opposition being the Communists.

Persecution of Christians eased

Churches can now be registered and Nepalis can become Christians legally. It is still, however, against the law to proselytise. Christians are much freer to practise their religion. There are now over 100,000 Christians, most with strong evangelistic zeal. There are now churches springing up all over the country. There are flourishing Bible correspondence courses and several new Bible schools. The Nepali church is said to be one of the fastest growing churches in the world, with a vision to plant a church in every village by the year 2,000.

Paimey

Prabhu Dan and Jyote are still running the dispensary. The Medical need is not so acute, as the road now comes within four or five hours' walk from the dispensary. The young people have done well in their exams. Some are thinking about how they can help their village with the dispensary and the church in the future.

Pastor Narhu is still in charge of the church, which is growing steadily. A long-standing problem over land for the church has at last been settled to the great delight of everyone.

Prem

In the 1960s a man named Gopal took a brave step in becoming the first man to be baptised in the hill village of Paimey. It was particularly brave as his father-in-law was a witch doctor, who then brought the full force of this craft to bear upon Gopal and his family. Gopal's wife had a mental breakdown from which she has not yet recovered, and his three sisters-in-law, who became Christians, all died quickly in unusual circumstances.

Shortly after Gopal and his wife were baptised they had a new baby. Some months later a couple, Paul and Rosalind, visited us from England. Seeing the baby tied on his mother's back, Rosalind asked his name. Gopal and his wife looked embarrassed and said, 'Well, we haven't actually given him a name. He was born on Tuesday, so we called him Tuesday.' We suddenly realised that those two were caught between two systems. In Hinduism it was the Brahman priest who gave the baby its name; the parents wouldn't think of doing so, although quite a lot of children got 'nicknames' by which they were called later. At that time we didn't have a pastor, so the baby had not been given a name.

I said, without thinking, you had better call him Paul, to the delight of the visiting Paul. This small incident would forge a future bond between the two Pauls and also with an older brother, Prem. It was this Prem that I visited in Moscow on my way to Nepal recently. He is a keen Christian, studying to be a doctor. He passed his first medical exam shortly before I arrived, having learned Russian for five months—he got a good pass mark! What a change in a generation: Gopal, the father, had never had the opportunity to go to school and still can't read or write.

Purna Maya

Just before taking her school-leaving certificate, Purna Maya went home to see her parents. Her father greeted her with the news that she was to be married the next day to a man she had never seen. She wrote, 'It was a surprise to me!' A Nepali pastor had come looking for a bride for his son, who was in the British Gurkhas and was shortly leaving for Hong Kong. Purna Maya's parents couldn't miss this opportunity to provide their daughter a life without hardship. To become or to marry a British Gurkha soldier is one of the greatest desires of any hill Nepali. Purna Maya did not demur but accepted the arranged marriage. Needless to say, I felt concerned for her. She and her husband had less than a week together before he was posted overseas. She went on and took her school-leaving certificate and started her nursing training. Recently I was delighted to be greeted by her in Pokhara, and she said to me, 'Aunty, God has given my husband and me such a deep love for each other. Maybe this arranged marriage was arranged in heaven!'

Promise

I am thankful for the privilege of living and working in the kingdom of Nepal. I rejoice in the new freedom and opportunities that Nepalis now have. God has said, 'I know what you do; I know you have a little power; you have followed my teaching and have been faithful to me. I have opened a door in front of you which no-one can close' (Rev 3:8). This has been true for me, and now has become true for many of my Nepali friends. The door in Nepal is truly open; may many more Nepalis enter it and find Christ. Will you help them to do so?